GET THIS
PARTY STARTED

To Meribeth,

For the priceless support
you gave me while I developed
this project, I can't begin
to tell you how much it meant to
me. Now let's take our
country back!

With love,
[signature]

GET THIS
PARTY STARTED

How Progressives
Can Fight Back and Win

Edited by Matthew R. Kerbel

Rowman & Littlefield Publishers, Inc.
Lanham • Boulder • New York • Toronto • Oxford

ROWMAN & LITTLEFIELD PUBLISHERS, INC.

Published in the United States of America
by Rowman & Littlefield Publishers, Inc.
A wholly owned subsidiary of The Rowman & Littlefield Publishing Group, Inc.
4501 Forbes Boulevard, Suite 200, Lanham, Maryland 20706
www.rowmanlittlefield.com

P.O. Box 317, Oxford OX2 9RU, UK

Distributed by NATIONAL BOOK NETWORK

British Library Cataloguing in Publication Information Available

Library of Congress Cataloging-in-Publication Data
Get this party started : how progressives can fight back and win /
edited by Matthew R. Kerbel.
    p. cm.
  Includes bibliographical references and index.
  ISBN 0-7425-4036-7 (cloth : alk. paper) — ISBN 0-7425-4037-5 (pbk. : alk. paper)
  1. Democratic Party (U.S.) 2. Progressivism (United States politics) 3. United
States—Politics and government—2001- I. Kerbel, Matthew Robert, 1958-
JK2316.G35 2006
324.2736—dc22

                                                                    2005022572

Printed in the United States of America

♾™ The paper used in this publication meets the minimum requirements of
American National Standard for Information Sciences—Permanence of Paper for
Printed Library Materials, ANSI/NISO Z39.48-1992.

For John White,
who provided the inspiration

CONTENTS

Foreword

LET'S GET TO WORK

Howard Dean

Throughout our history, progressives have been the primary force for compassion and opportunity in society and have helped to improve the lives of Americans from improved education and health care to better working conditions and strong economic growth with fiscal responsibility. But Democrats have not learned until now how to effectively be in the minority. It is as if we got punched in the nose in a playground fight by a bully and then forgot how to defend ourselves and our country. Somehow we forgot that people who behave like the right wing are not nice people and that we'll have to be a lot tougher and smarter than we have been to take back the America we grew up in.

This book features a lot of information from some tough, smart, and often young people about how to get our side in shape to take on bullies again, both at home and abroad: say what you believe, tell the truth, organize, trust local people, pay attention to the American people, don't talk down to voters, get outside of Washington, and don't be afraid to talk about moral values, because ours are closer to mainstream American values than the values of the right wing. Above all, fight. Fight like your own life and the lives of your children depend on winning, because it's true.

If America is to succeed as a nation, the progressive impulse must succeed first. This book offers some solid, practical advice about how to succeed in a world where politics is a lot dirtier and tougher than ever before. It's also a world where politics matters a lot more than it used to.

Americans want a change, and only progressives can provide it. The conservative role in our nation's history has most often been to slow down and consolidate change, while the progressive role has been to accelerate change and find new directions.

Americans want fairness, opportunity, and strong world leadership. Only a vibrant progressive movement with democratic values can deliver that. The path to revitalizing this movement—to getting this party started—is outlined in the pages ahead. We know what needs to be done. Now let's get to work.

Preface

MERGING MESSAGE, ELECTORAL, AND ORGANIZATIONAL STRATEGIES

Matthew R. Kerbel

The purpose of this book is to provide focus and direction to the ongoing debate over what progressives in general and Democrats in particular must do to reemerge as a dominant force in national politics, rising not only from the ashes of our most recent electoral defeat but from the debilitating effects of being beaten down for over a decade by a determined, disciplined, and sometimes brutal Republican juggernaut. Considering that Democrats narrowly but thoroughly lost what pollster John Zogby ominously labeled "the Armageddon election" of 2004, the discussion among Democrats about how to proceed in the wake of John Kerry's defeat has been remarkably civil. It's not difficult to imagine a high level of acrimony coming from across the aisle if, by virtue of a shift in the preferences of some 60,000 Ohioans, a Republican strategy that ignored the political center at the expense of boosting turnout among their base had resulted in Electoral College defeat. Ours is a system where the winner takes all the representation, even if by the narrowest of margins, and the loser gets all the recrimination. Under the circumstances, as well as by historical standards, Democrats have been doing a pretty good job of soldiering on.

Still, the discussion of what to do next has a fragmented quality. Some people focus on message strategies, debating what Democrats should stand for and say. Others focus on electoral strategies, debating which constituencies need to be massaged. Still others focus on organizational strategies, debating the best ways to engage supporters and boost turnout. In truth, each of these is an important component of building a lasting progressive majority, and each works with the others. This book brings together leading progressive voices in an integrated discussion of the message, electoral, and organizational strategies Democrats should pursue as they sort through the wreckage of the 2004 election.

Washington Post columnist E. J. Dionne initiates the discussion by laying out the competing concerns and demands of Democrats as they reacted to Kerry's defeat and arrived at a host of often contradictory conclusions about what to do next. His retrospective take on the election is followed by a look at the reasons why Kerry lost by scholar and blogger Alan Abramowitz, who finds surprising lessons in the election data that upend conventional wisdom about the Republican's ability to drive up turnout among religious conservatives and about the supposed shortcomings of the Democrat's get-out-the-vote initiatives. His is also a cautionary tale about the Democrats' national security problems, an ongoing issue that pollster Anna Greenberg discusses in the context of one of the little noticed but potentially critical trends of the past two election cycles: the shrinking of the gender gap.

The next three essays advocate moving away from the false ideological debate surrounding whether Democrats need to be "more liberal" or move "closer to the center" in favor of a values-based agenda rooted in long-held progressive beliefs. John Kenneth White, who analyzed 2004 campaign data for John Zogby and who has written extensively on the values divide between the "red" and "blue" states, explains why progressives tend to think programmatically while voters think thematically, and calls for progressives to connect with voters while remaining true to core beliefs. Activist, commentator, and best-selling author Jim Wallis takes up that call, articulating a moral agenda of personal responsibility and social justice true to progressive values that would resonate with voters who are turned off by the ideological polarization of the parties. Former Clinton chief of staff John Podesta and John Halpin, both of the Center for American Progress, trace the successful history of progressive politics in the twentieth century and demonstrate how progressive values can infuse a policy agenda built around the principles of fairness, global leadership, and community. One element of their agenda is political reform—long a progressive hallmark, and a topic addressed by Craig Holman, legislative representative for the consumer advocacy organization Public Citizen, who explains why closing the loophole that leaves Section 527 groups free to raise and spend unlimited sums of money amounts to good policy and good politics for reform-minded progressives.

Value-laden issues of what progressives need to say go hand in hand with the practical question of how to they should say it. George Lakoff, professor of linguistics at Berkeley and founding senior fellow of the Rockridge Institute, offers advice on how progressives can frame the political debate in terms that will make it possible to win. Author and former Clinton speechwriter David Kusnet follows with advice on what progressives can learn from George W. Bush about how to speak to an American audience.

As E. J. Dionne says in his chapter, "Organization without a cause is sterile. But a cause without organization is hopeless." In a search for hope, the final three contributors discuss how the Democratic Party can overcome its organizational woes and advance the agenda detailed earlier in the book. All find cause for optimism in the grass roots of the Democratic Party. *Washington Monthly* editor Amy Sullivan takes on the Beltway consultant class and suggests Democrats should stop rewarding political consultants who keep losing elections. Her notion that hitherto unknown consultants will emerge—if encouraged to do so—from successful state and local races complements the potential that Zephyr Teachout finds in the Internet to serve as a tool for organizing disparate supporters of progressive candidates. From her vantage point as a consultant and former head of Internet outreach for Howard Dean's presidential campaign, Teachout contends that campaign consultants on the left and right still do not understand how to put the Internet to work for maximum gain and offers an approach to Internet organizing that could greatly benefit the Democratic Party and its candidates. Her chapter is followed by a discussion from Chris Bowers of the popular progressive weblog MyDD on how "blogs" can be a critically important tool for progressives in a rapidly changing news environment.

The book closes with my observations on how these chapters, taken together, can provide a practical plan of action for Democratic elites and grassroots supporters of progressive politics.

One final note: although the contributors to this volume alternately and interchangeably discuss Democrats and progressives, clearly not all Democrats are progressives and not all progressives are Democrats. The distinction—or lack thereof—is clouded by the emergence of parties that more closely follow ideological agendas than at any time in recent memory and by the fact that the Democratic Party remains the largest viable vehicle for progressive political engagement. To those who might be offended by conflating the two, please accept my apology. At this point in history, the number of people taking offense to merging Democrats with progressives is probably very small, which speaks to the degree of unity expressed by Democrats at the national and grassroots levels and by progressives everywhere and is a sign of the willingness and determination of those in the 48.3 percent of the electorate who did not receive any representation following the last election to make lasting changes. In that spirit and to that end, it is my hope that the discussion in the pages that follow will provide a focal point for developing a blueprint for a progressive era.

I

GETTING OFF
THE ROAD TO NOWHERE

E. J. Dionne

In recent months, I've had conversations with just about every kind of Democrat, each as certain and as passionate as the next about what the party's top priorities should be. How can Democratic National Committee Chairman Howard Dean, or anyone, square all these disparate imperatives, one with the other? Alternatively, can Dean choose some and reject others without a lot of Democrats screaming?

The must-do list included:

1. Defeating the Bush Social Security plan;
2. Establishing the Democrats as strong, tough, and trustworthy in fighting terrorism and pursuing a responsible foreign policy;
3. Asserting the party's identification with moral values and religion;
4. Holding fast to the party's commitment to abortion rights and tolerance;
5. Crafting an economic message to bring back socially conservative but financially pressed voters;
6. Reinvigorating the party's organization to match Karl Rove's Republican machine, state by state, precinct by precinct;
7. Building on the work in 2004 of outside groups such as MoveOn.org and America Coming Together, because the old party politics are irrelevant to the future;

8. Standing for something even if it's unfashionable—such as the erad-
   ication of poverty—because voters are looking for strength and commitment, and don't like candidates who speak Focusgroupese;
9. Understanding the views of NASCAR dads, security moms, country-
   western music fans, gun owners, Southerners, country people, and
   others who regard the Democrats as the party of overeducated, arrogant, Volvo-driving elitists.

And that is just a partial catalogue.

Of course, it's possible for advocates of Priority No. 5 (having a clear
economic message), to join forces with those pushing Priority No. 9
(reaching out to NASCAR dads and gun owners). But the many obvious
tensions in the list speak to the very peculiar and difficult nature of the
party's post–2004 debate.

Because the 2004 election was so close, almost anything any Democrat says about why President Bush won reelection can be true. It's perfectly possible to see the party as being in fine shape, that it was hard to
beat a wartime incumbent, that the Democrats need only a few more
percentage points to be back on top. It's equally plausible to argue that
the party must be in awful shape if it couldn't defeat Bush after the job
losses of his first four years and the problematic Iraq war.

It's also possible to blame the defeat on John Kerry's personal shortcomings. It's just as legitimate to argue that many of Kerry's difficulties—
his ambivalent position on the war in Iraq, his cautious campaign—
reflected a deeper defect in a party that can't quite figure out what it
stands for.

It's stunning that a year after Dean's crash-and-burn exit from the
presidential race he emerged as the top candidate to lead the party back
to glory. His victory is the result, in part, of his shrewd understanding of
the politics of the 447-member Democratic National Committee. But
there was another reason for Dean's comeback: He appeared to be in
the best position to meet most—though not all—of the competing demands of Democratic activists.

He'll need to be very pragmatic. Hawkish Democrats were initially
alarmed at the rise of the antiwar, sometimes loose-talking Dean; Southerners and more socially conservative Democrats wonder what good a
Yale graduate from Vermont can possibly do for their party.

But the very fact that Dean sought the job—can you remember any failed presidential candidate who went on to be Democratic Party chairman?—suggests that he understands that at this moment of highly polarized politics, leading the opposition party's formal organization is potentially one of the most powerful positions in American politics.

Few see the potential of Dean's chairmanship better than Simon Rosenberg, who sought the job but dropped out in the face of Dean's juggernaut. Rosenberg is a perfect political hybrid: He heads up the centrist New Democrat Network and has developed a deep respect for the world of Internet politics and the way Dean used the new technology in 2004.

"People don't understand how disproportionately important the Democratic National Committee is going to be in driving politics for Democrats," Rosenberg says. "We used to have precinct captains and county chairmen: Your relationship to the party was brokered by many intermediaries. Now, there are millions of Americans who have a direct relationship with the national party which is more meaningful than their relationship with their local party." If you doubt that, compare how much money was raised for national Democrats online, and how much was delivered by the remains of the old local party organizations.

As party chairman, Rosenberg argues, Dean will have direct access to those millions of Democrats through e-mail and more control over the Democratic "brand" than any congressional leader could hope to enjoy. But what, exactly, will he do with it? Much depends on how he and the party settle two core arguments about the need to oppose versus the need to offer alternatives and about ideas versus organization.

THE NEED TO OPPOSE VS. THE NEED TO OFFER ALTERNATIVES

Newt Gingrich may be an odd Democratic hero, but the genius of the former Speaker's take-no-prisoners politics is now the hottest talking point in Democratic politics. Gingrich relished the role of opposition leader in Bill Clinton's first term: He fought down Clinton's health care bill, making the rookie president look like a failure. He undercut Clinton's crime bill, which was supposed to be a moderate, "New Democrat" approach, by making it look like a package of liberal social programs. And he was unrelenting in attacking the ethics of Democratic leaders. Democrats eager to use ethics issues against House Majority Leader Tom DeLay are closely studying the Gingrich script.

There is no bigger target for Democrats than Bush's partial privatization plan for Social Security. Opposing Bush's approach gives something to every Democratic faction. Moderates hate the huge borrowing the proposal entails. Liberals cannot abide turning away from the idea of social insurance at the heart of the New Deal. Democrats of all stripes think Bush is exaggerating the immediacy of the problem. And from bitter experience, Democrats know that there is no political percentage in playing ball with Bush, since he has shown he will work hard to defeat any vulnerable Democrat, even those who have supported him on many issues.

Opposing Bush isn't just a liberal preoccupation now. It's a Democratic preoccupation. "Bush's extremism unifies Democrats," says Robert Borosage, a founder of the liberal Campaign for America's Future, "so the fault lines are beneath that."

But is opposition a better way to go than offering alternatives? That question will be easier to resolve if it is recognized as a classic false choice. As Borosage notes, the differences among Democrats "aren't nearly as big as our differences with Bush." And it is important to remember that parties often define what they are *for* by being highly principled about what they are against. By opposing the expansion of slavery, Abraham Lincoln established himself as emphatically in favor of freedom. Precisely because Ronald Reagan defined himself as opposed to Communism and high taxes, no one had to ask if he had a "positive vision."

As Reagan understood better than anyone, the words of opposition must be accompanied by the music of aspiration. The critique of Bush's domestic agenda must rest on a sustained argument that if enacted, the president's program would set back great goals—social justice, opportunity, community, public service—that must be advanced through alternative policies. Thus, Democrats must make clear that they oppose Bush's tax cuts for the wealthy *not* because they hate the rich, but because a well-functioning government can expand opportunities for those who otherwise would have little chance for the ownership promised by Bush's "ownership society."

The Democrats' greatest challenge will be to create an alternative foreign policy that has credibility with those outside the party while uniting those within it. You don't have to be a hawk to agree with Democrat Will Marshall, of the centrist Progressive Policy Institute, when he points to polls showing that Democrats have lagged behind Republicans on national security questions since the 1970s. He argues that the party prospered in the 1990s in large part because foreign policy declined as a voting issue.

Kerry tried to thread the needle in 2004 by opposing Bush's approach while insisting that he, too, would be tough on terrorism. It didn't work. On this question, Dean may have a Nixon–to–China opportunity: As a leader with credibility among the party's doves, he may be well placed to bring together the party's feuding factions to create a tough internationalism that is the only plausible counter to Bush's approach. This task is political, but also intellectual and moral, and one the party cannot evade.

Advocates of the "alternatives" route need to remember how tough Bill Clinton, the king of new ideas, was in attacking the first President Bush on economics, foreign policy—and just about everything else. Advocates of opposition know that down the road, the party will need some galvanizing ideas to convince the undecided that Democrats are serious about governing. Remember, Newt Gingrich followed up his successful opposition tactics with the "Contract With America."

IDEAS VS. ORGANIZATION

But really, how important are ideas? Was it George Bush's ideas that won in 2004? Or was it Karl Rove and Ken Mehlman's exceptional organization of local precincts, conservative churches, business groups, gun owners, abortion foes, and Hollywood haters?

Organization without a cause is sterile. But a cause without organization is hopeless. Democrats need to ask themselves some very hard questions—hard, because parts of the party won't like the answers. For example, the party needs to revive its state organizations, but some states have such poor organizations that investing in them will just be throwing money away. For all the talk about the GOP having stronger local parties, the Republican grassroots effort in 2004 was largely built by the national party and national fundraising efforts.

It's not just the old Democratic machines that are moribund or nonexistent. The party's most important allies, the unions, are as weak as they have been in decades. Republicans, meanwhile, can rely on national networks that are rooted locally: conservative churches especially, but also small business groups, gun clubs, and various "family values" organizations.

Do the long-term trends favor the Republicans or the Democrats? The answer is by no means obvious.

On the one hand: The Republicans are doing very well in many of the nation's growing outer suburbs, and conservative churches are more engaged in politics than ever. Meanwhile, the blue states in the Northeast and Midwest have, over several decades, seen their populations and electoral clout shrink relative to other parts of the country.

On the other hand: Social attitudes on all manner of issues, including gay rights, are more liberal than they used to be. Rural America, a great source of strength for Bush, is losing electoral clout. Voters under 30 were the one age group Kerry carried. It's unusual for the losing candidate to win the youngest voters, a heartening sign for the Democrats' future.

As they face that future, Democrats should not be ashamed of learning from George Bush. Bush has been a genius not only at mobilizing his party's base but also at nickel-and-diming the Democrats by stealing pieces of the old Democratic constituencies. He wooed more conservative Catholics and turned a small Democratic Catholic advantage into a small Republican one. He pulled over more Hispanic voters, even if the exact size of the GOP gains is a matter of hot dispute. He used national security issues to cut the Democrats' advantage among women.

Bush won reelection for many reasons, but one of them was that he conveyed a sense that he knew where he wanted to take the country, and why. Bush cut into Democratic constituencies not by pretending that he was a Democrat, but by appealing to their social conservatism or their hawkishness on foreign policy. The appeal to these swing groups—it will pain Democrats to hear this—was rooted in principle.

Democratic leaders are under tremendous pressure from the competing factions of the must-do crowd. Rank-and-file Democrats yearn to fight for things that matter and to stand for more than just what consultants tell them they should say. Democrats know this period of time will be a hell of a ride, but they're willing to take some risks to get off the road to nowhere.

2

EXPLAINING BUSH'S VICTORY IN 2004 (IT'S TERRORISM, STUPID!)

Alan I. Abramowitz

In 2004, for the first time since 1928, a Republican president was re-elected along with Republican majorities in the Senate and House of Representatives. President Bush's margins in both the popular and the electoral vote were relatively narrow. Mr. Bush won 50.7 percent of the popular vote and 286 electoral votes to 48.3 percent of the popular vote and 252 electoral votes for his Democratic challenger, Massachusetts Senator John Kerry. Despite the closeness of the election, however, the fact that Mr. Bush was the first presidential candidate to win a majority of the popular vote since his father in 1988, the Republican gains in the Senate and House of Representatives, and a dramatic increase in voter turnout have fueled speculation that this was an extraordinary election with potentially long-lasting consequences for American politics.

Some conservative strategists and pundits have argued that the 2004 results may solidify Republican domination of Congress and the presidency. Republican National Committee Chairman Ken Mehlman recently claimed, "The Republican Party is in a stronger position today than at any time since the Great Depression." In Mehlman's view, "Something fundamental and significant happened in this election that creates an opportunity" for the Republican Party to maintain and extend its gains in future elections.[1]

According to Mehlman and other conservative commentators, George Bush's victory in 2004, along with GOP gains in the House and Senate, reflected a successful two-pronged strategy: (1) emphasizing the need for strong leadership to counter the threat of terrorism, and (2) mobilizing millions of evangelical Christians and other culturally conservative voters upset about gay marriage, abortion, and other threats to traditional values. By aggressively pursuing the war on terrorism and by enacting policies such as a constitutional amendment prohibiting gay marriage, these conservatives now believe that President Bush and Congress can solidify the Republicans' newly expanded base and ensure GOP control of Congress and the White House for years to come. Some scholars appear to agree with this assessment. Walter Dean Burnham, one of the nation's leading experts on past party realignments, recently observed, "If Republicans keep playing the religious card along with the terrorism card, this could last a long time."[2]

Of course, not everyone accepts the argument that the 2004 election signaled a fundamental shift in support for the Democratic and Republican parties. Liberal political analysts such as Ruy Teixeira of the Center for American Progress, while acknowledging the significance of Republican victories in the presidential and congressional elections, tend to emphasize the limited nature of the GOP's gains and attribute Bush's reelection mainly to the skillful use of incumbency in a time of war. According to Teixeira, it's hard to read the results in a serious way as a mandate for much of anything. Similarly, according to political scientist Larry Bartels of Princeton University, the level of support for Republican candidates by culturally conservative white voters in 2004 was similar to that seen in other recent elections and did not signal a major shift within the electorate.[3]

It may take years to determine whether the 2004 election signaled the beginning of a new era of Republican domination of American politics or was simply a normal election in an era of intense competition for the support of a closely divided electorate. However, data already available suggest that Republican claims that 2004 was a landmark election are overstated and raise serious doubts about the notion that Republicans won the election on the strength of a massive turnout of social conservatives. In this chapter I address the effects of national security issues, social issues, and incumbency on the 2004 election by examining evidence from the election results and data from the 2004 national exit poll and the 2004 American National Election Study. The good news for Democrats is that Republican success in mobilizing evangelical Christians in 2004 was matched by Democratic success in mobilizing African-Americans and college students. Moreover, the GOP message of strong leadership in a time of war was magnified by an incumbency effect that is not transferable to the next Republican nominee. However, there is also an important cautionary note to Democrats about their continuing disadvantage on national security issues, especially with swing voters who, contrary to the current conventional wisdom, still can make or break the fortunes of presidential candidates.

VOTER TURNOUT

About 122.2 million Americans voted in the 2004 presidential election, an increase of almost 17 million compared with the 105.4 million who voted in the 2000 presidential election. Even so, the estimated turnout of eligible voters in 2004 was only 60 percent, up from 54.2 percent in 2000, but below the 60.6 percent turnout in 1992 and below turnout rates for all three of the presidential elections during the 1960s.[4]

A more important question about voter turnout in the 2004 election is who voted. Did the Republican Party in fact mobilize millions of evangelical Christians by emphasizing its opposition to gay marriage? Certainly one key element in the Republicans' "gay marriage strategy" involved the placement of antigay marriage referenda on the ballot in eleven states in an attempt to increase turnout among evangelicals and other social conservatives who would also vote for George Bush and Republican congressional candidates.

An examination of state turnout data suggests, however, that the strategy of using gay marriage referenda to increase turnout was ineffective. In the eleven states with gay marriage referenda on the ballot, turnout of eligible voters increased by an average of 5.1 percentage points, from 55.9 percent in 2000 to 61.0 percent in 2004. In the rest of the country, turnout increased by an average of 4.4 percentage points, from 57.3 percent in 2000 to 61.7 percent in 2004. Moreover, a multiple regression analysis of statewide turnout in 2004 shows that the presence of gay marriage referenda on the ballot had no impact on turnout. Based on the results, the strongest predictor of turnout in 2004 was turnout in 2000. In addition, twelve swing states—the states that were heavily contested by both presidential candidates until the end of the campaign— saw their turnout rates increase by a statistically significant 3.7 points beyond what was predicted based on their turnout levels in 2000, and nine states with hotly contested Senate races saw a more modest increase in turnout of just over one percentage point. However, turnout in states with gay marriage referenda on the ballot was no higher than expected.

If gay marriage referenda had no discernible impact on turnout, the dramatic increase in swing state turnout suggests that voter registration and get-out-the-vote drives conducted by both major parties and affiliated groups, which were heavily concentrated in swing states, were effective in getting voters to the polls. Data from the 2004 American National Election Study allow us to explore this point. Table 2.1 displays the relationship between turnout and voter recollection of having been contacted by party or nonparty groups, controlling for family income, education, and party identification.

The results indicate that get-out-the-vote drives were effective in increasing turnout, and that the effect was much greater among groups

Table 2.1. Turnout Percentages among Voters Recalling and Not Recalling Pre-election Contact in the 2004 Presidential Election

Voter Group	Cannot Recall Contact (%)	Recall Contact (%)	Difference
Family Income			
Less than $25,000	50	83	+33
$25,000–$49,999	59	89	+30
$50,000–$89,999	79	93	+14
$90,000 or More	86	91	+5
Education			
High School Only	52	84	+32
Some College	69	90	+21
College Graduates	88	96	+8
Party Identification			
Democrats	69	89	+20
Independents	50	84	+34
Republicans	82	95	+13

Source: 2004 American National Election Study

that normally turn out at a relatively low rate than among groups that normally turn out at a relatively high rate, a pattern that generally favors Democrats. Thus, the difference in reported turnout between those who recalled being contacted and those who did not was 33 percentage points among lower-income citizens but only 5 percentage points among upper-income citizens, and 32 percentage points among the high school educated but only 8 percentage points among college graduates. As a result, these data indicate that get-out-the-vote contacts had a greater impact on turnout among independents (a 34 percentage point difference) and Democrats (a 20 percentage point difference) than among Republicans (a 13 percentage point difference).

THE 2004 ELECTION AS A
REFERENDUM ON GEORGE BUSH

How surprising was George Bush's victory in the 2004 presidential election? The answer, based on the historical record, is not surprising at all. Incumbent presidents usually win. In the century preceding the 2004 election, twenty incumbent presidents sought reelection and fifteen were successful, for a reelection rate of 75 percent. Moreover, incumbent presidents like George Bush whose party has held the White House for only one term do even better.[5] In the past century, ten of eleven such first-term presidents have been reelected; the only failure was Jimmy Carter in 1980. Viewed in this context, Bush's performance was the worst of any successful incumbent during this time, as he received the smallest share of both the popular and electoral vote of any reelected first-term incumbent since 1900.

Was George Bush's victory the result of a brilliantly planned and executed campaign strategy and/or a deeply flawed strategy on the part of the Kerry campaign? If so, one would expect to find that Bush did substantially better than he should have done based on his level of public support before the main phase of the general election campaign began. But he didn't. Figure 2.1 shows the results of a regression analysis of the vote received by all ten incumbent presidents since World War II based on their net approval rating (percent approving minus percent disapproving) in the final Gallup poll in June of the election year, before the fall campaign had begun. These data show a fairly strong relationship between a president's approval rating in June and his vote in November. However, the relationship is not perfect. Some presidents, like Richard Nixon and Ronald Reagan, do somewhat better than expected, perhaps because their popularity increased during the campaign or they faced weak challengers. Other presidents, like Dwight Eisenhower and Gerald Ford, do a little worse than expected. But the point for George W. Bush falls right on the regression line. Bush did exactly as well as expected based on his approval rating in June. There is no indication here that the election outcome reflected a brilliantly executed campaign by the Republicans or a flawed campaign by the Democrats. Rather, the outcome of the 2004 presidential election reflected established divisions within the electorate over President Bush and his policies.

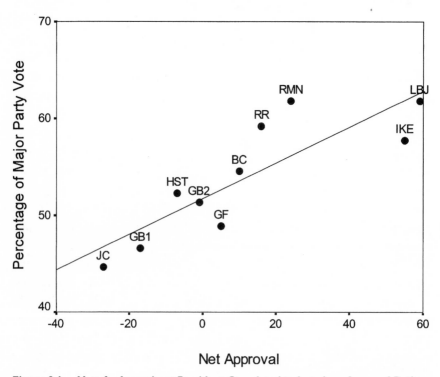

Figure 2.1.   Vote for Incumbent President Correlated to Late June Approval Ratings
Legend: BC = Bill Clinton; GB1 = George H. W. Bush; GB2 = George W. Bush; GF = Gerald Ford; HST = Harry S Truman; IKE = Dwight Eisenhower; JC = Jimmy Carter; LBJ = Lyndon Johnson; RMN = Richard Nixon; RR = Ronald Reagan.

The 2004 presidential election was largely a referendum on the performance of President Bush, and voters were almost evenly divided in
their assessment of that performance. According to the national exit
poll, 22 percent of voters were "enthusiastic" about the Bush administration, 26 percent were "satisfied," 26 percent were "dissatisfied," and
23 percent were "angry." The overwhelming majority of those who were
enthusiastic or satisfied voted for the president, while the overwhelming
majority of those who were dissatisfied or angry voted against the president. Opinions about Mr. Bush fell largely along party lines and showed
little change during the campaign. In fact, they were almost identical to
opinions about Mr. Bush in the aftermath of the disputed 2000 election
and before the September 11, 2001, terrorist attacks.

THE 2004 ELECTION AS A RERUN OF THE 2000 ELECTION

The results of the 2004 presidential election also closely reflected the
results of the 2000 presidential election. Despite all that transpired in
the interim—the terrorist attacks, a controversial war in Iraq, a surge in
unemployment, and the reemergence of large federal budget deficits—
only three small states switched sides between 2000 and 2004: New
Hampshire went from the Republican column to the Democratic, while
Iowa and New Mexico went from the Democratic column to the Republican. And, in all three states, the race was extremely close in both
2000 and 2004.

Figure 2.2 shows that there was a very strong relationship between
the results of the 2000 and 2004 presidential elections across all of the
states. George Bush ran slightly ahead of his 2000 percentage in almost
every state. He gained an average of 2.6 percentage points in states that
he carried four years earlier and 2.8 percentage points in states that Al
Gore carried four years earlier. He gained an average of 2.7 percentage
points in states with below-average unemployment and 2.6 percentage
points in states with above-average unemployment. He gained an average of 2.5 percentage points in states with gay marriage referenda on the
ballot and 2.7 percentage points in states without such referenda. There
was one localized exception to this pattern: the incumbent gained an average of 5.4 percentage points in the three states most directly affected

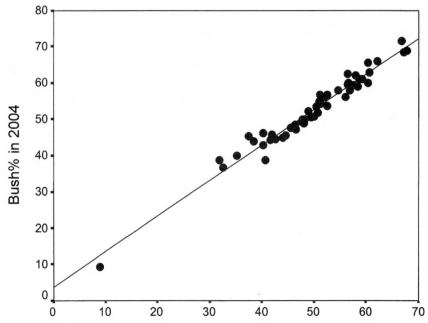

Figure 2.2.   Percentage of the Vote for Bush in 2004 Correlated to Percentage of the Vote for Bush in 2000, by State

by the September 11 terrorist attacks—New York, New Jersey, and Connecticut—compared with 2.5 percentage points in the rest of the country.

A regression analysis of George Bush's percentage of the state-by-state vote in 2004, as influenced by a series of factors that could have affected the outcome (the presence of gay marriage ballot referenda, statewide unemployment rates, Bush's statewide share of the 2000 vote, and the direct experience of a terrorist attack in the three states of the New York metropolitan area)[6] demonstrates that by far the strongest predictor of Bush's vote in 2004 was his vote in 2000. It confirms that gay marriage referenda had no impact on the results and that Bush did significantly better than expected in the three states most directly affected by September 11. It also indicates that state unemployment rates did not influence Bush's share of the vote.

However, the level of voter turnout in a state did make a difference—and not in the direction suggested by analysts who attribute Bush's victory to an effective get-out-the-vote campaign. Turnout had a significant and negative impact on Bush's vote—the president did better than expected in states with relatively low levels of turnout and worse than expected in states with relatively high levels of turnout after controlling for his performance in those states four years earlier. According to the American National Election Study data examined earlier in this chapter, voter registration and get-out-the-vote campaigns had a greater impact on lower socioeconomic status voters, independents, and Democrats than on upper socioeconomic status voters and Republicans. Whatever success the Republican campaign had in mobilizing conservative evangelicals and other pro-Bush voters was apparently more than offset by the success of the Democratic campaign in mobilizing African-Americans, college students, and other anti-Bush voters.

These results do lend a bit of support to the effectiveness of one part of the Republican strategy in the 2004 election, however. The fact that George Bush did significantly better than expected in the three states most affected by the events of September 11, 2001, speaks to the efficacy of emphasizing the president's leadership in the war on terrorism while raising doubts about John Kerry's ability to deal effectively with the terrorist threat. Although Bush lost all three of these states by wide margins, the issue of terrorism probably contributed to the small gains that the president made in the rest of the country.

THE PARTISAN DIVIDE

There was very little change in the party loyalties of the American electorate between 2000 and 2004. Table 2.2 compares the distribution of party identification among registered voters nationwide in 2004 with the comparable distribution in 2000, according to the National Annenberg Election Surveys.[7] There is almost no difference between the two distributions. Democrats enjoyed a three-point advantage in party identification in 2004 and a four-point advantage in 2000. There were also slightly fewer independent voters in 2004 than in 2000.[8]

The stability of party identification in the national electorate between 2000 and 2004 helps to explain the tremendous continuity between the results of these two elections at the local, state, and national levels,

Table 2.2.   Party Identification of Registered Voters in 2000 and 2004

Party Identification	2000 (%)	2004 (%)	Change (%)
Democratic	34	35	+1
Republican	30	32	+2
Independent and Other	36	33	−3

Source: National Annenberg Election Surveys
Note: 2004 results based on interviews with 67,777 registered voters between October 7, 2003, and November 16, 2004. 2000 results based on interviews with 44,877 registered voters between December 14, 1999, and January 19, 2001.

because both of these contests produced very high levels of party voting. Table 2.3 displays the relationship between party identification and presidential voting with data from the 2004 American National Election Study. According to the data in this table, 95 percent of voters in 2004 expressed some degree of attachment to one of the two major parties and the overwhelming majority of these voters supported their own party's nominee: 91 percent of strong, weak, and independent Democrats voted for John Kerry, while 92 percent of strong, weak, and independent Republicans voted for George Bush. These results are very similar to those from the 2004 national exit poll. According to the exit poll data, 89 percent of Democratic identifiers voted for John Kerry and 90 percent of Republican identifiers voted for George Bush.

The extraordinarily high level of partisan voting in recent presidential elections is due largely to the fact that a gradual ideological realignment has taken place among voters in the United States since the 1980s, with conservatives increasingly identifying with the Republican Party and liberals/progressives increasingly identifying with the Democratic Party.[9] One consequence of this realignment has been a dramatic reduction in the size of the overall Democratic advantage in party identi-

Table 2.3.   2004 Presidential Vote by Party Identification

	Democrats (%)	Independents[a] (%)	Republicans (%)
Voted for Kerry	91	58	8
Voted for Bush	9	42	92
Total	100	100	100
(n)	(370)	(41)	(365)

Source: 2004 American National Election Study
[a]Independents leaning toward a party are classified as Democrats or Republicans.

fication as conservative Democrats in the South and elsewhere shifted their allegiance to the Republicans. Another consequence has been that voters' party affiliations have become more consistent with their ideological orientations. According to data from the American National Election Study, liberal Democrats and conservative Republicans made up 42 percent of white party identifiers in 1972, while conservative Democrats and liberal Republicans made up 20 percent. By 2004, however, liberal Democrats and conservative Republicans accounted for 59 percent of white party identifiers, with conservative Democrats and liberal Republicans down to just 9 percent.

The growing consistency of ideology and party identification has important consequences for voting behavior, because voters whose party identification and ideological orientation are consistent are much more loyal to their party than voters whose party identification and ideological orientation are inconsistent. According to data from the national exit poll, 96 percent of liberal white Democrats voted for John Kerry, compared with only 62 percent of conservative white Democrats. Similarly, 97 percent of conservative white Republicans voted for George W. Bush, compared with only 58 percent of liberal white Republicans. Without question, the stability of this partisan/ideological divide is one of the defining characteristics of the current electoral environment.

SWING VOTERS IN 2004

Although voters whose partisan and ideological orientations are inconsistent now constitute a small minority of the electorate, conservative Democrats and moderate-to-liberal Republicans, along with the small group of voters who lack any party affiliation, can be considered swing voters in presidential elections because they are capable of supporting either party depending on their reactions to the candidates and issues. The importance of swing voters has been downplayed in the prevailing media narrative of the 2004 election, as President Bush is credited with boosting the turnout of his base to the exclusion of these voters in order to win reelection. Given the relatively close division of the electorate between core supporters of the two major parties, though, the way swing voters break can determine the outcome of a presidential election, especially if core supporters of both parties are highly motivated to turn out, as was the case in 2004.

Table 2.4 displays the presidential preferences of swing voters in elections from 1988 to 2004. Swing voters include conservative and independent-leaning Democrats; moderate, liberal, and independent-leaning Republicans; and pure independents. The data presented in this table indicate that these voters do indeed swing back and forth between the two parties from election to election. Moreover—and contrary to the analysis that says Bush won by relying on a large turnout from his base—the candidate supported by a majority or plurality of swing voters almost always wins the election.

In 1988, the large majority of swing voters supported the Republican candidate, George H. W. Bush, over his Democratic rival, Michael Dukakis, and Bush won a relatively easy victory in the election. In 1992, a large proportion of swing voters opted for independent candidate H. Ross Perot, leaving the Democratic challenger and eventual winner, Bill Clinton, with a narrow plurality of swing voters. Four years later, with Perot again in the race, swing voters chose Clinton over his Republican challenger, Bob Dole, and Clinton won reelection by a comfortable margin. In 2000 a majority of swing voters chose George W. Bush over Al Gore, a pattern that repeated itself in 2004, with a slightly larger majority of swing voters selecting Bush over John Kerry.

In order to determine what issues had the greatest influence on swing voters in the 2004 presidential election, I conducted a logistic regression analysis of the presidential vote among respondents in the 2004 Ameri-

Table 2.4. Candidate Preference of Swing Voters in Recent Presidential Elections

	Percentage Voting for		
Election	Democrat (%)	Republican (%)	Other (%)
1988	41	59	—
1992	37	35	28
1996	45	40	15
2000	46	54	—
2004	44	56	—

Source: American National Election Study
Note: Swing voters include conservative Democrats and leaning Democrats, moderate to liberal Republicans and leaning Republicans, and pure independents.

can National Election Study who were identified as swing voters: conservative Democratic identifiers and "leaners" who express a weak preference for the Democratic Party, moderate-to-liberal Republican identifiers and "leaners," and pure independents. The analysis takes into account their party identification and their ideological positioning on issues associated with New Deal liberalism (government responsibility for jobs and living standards, health insurance, government spending and services, and government aid to minorities), social issues (abortion and gay marriage), and national security issues (defense spending and the proper role of diplomacy vs. military force in foreign policy).

The results of the analysis show that national security issues were much more important to swing voters in the 2004 presidential election than either traditional New Deal issues or social issues.[10] Moreover, the attitudes of swing voters on national security issues set them apart from the electorate as a whole. Table 2.5 compares the attitudes of swing voters with those of all voters in the 2004 American National Election Study on a variety of domestic and foreign policy issues. The data in this table show that swing voters had similar attitudes to the rest of the electorate on social issues such as abortion and gay marriage. In addition, a majority of swing voters, along with a majority of all voters, disapproved of President Bush's handling of the economy, the federal budget deficit, and the war in Iraq. On all of these issues, the attitudes of swing voters toward the president's policies were either similar to—or more negative

Table 2.5.   Attitudes of Swing Voters in 2004

	All Voters (%)	Swing Voters (%)
Pro-Choice	55	60
Pro-Gay Marriage	32	30
Approve Bush's Handling of		
Budget Deficit	35	34
Economy	44	46
War in Iraq	44	44
Foreign Relations	45	52
War on Terror	56	64
Party Preferred on Terrorism		
Democrats	26	16
Republicans	45	47

Source: 2004 American National Election Study
Note: Swing voters include conservative Democrats and leaning Democrats, moderate to liberal Republicans and leaning Republicans, and pure independents.

than—the attitudes of the overall electorate. On the issues of foreign policy and terrorism, however, swing voters had more favorable opinions of the president's policies than the rest of the electorate and on the question of which party could better handle the problem of terrorism, swing voters preferred the GOP to the Democrats by a decisive 3 to 1 margin.

The main difference between swing voters and the overall electorate on this question was in the percentage trusting Democrats to keep them safe. Not only did opinions on national security issues have a much stronger influence on the candidate preference of swing voters than either New Deal issues or social issues, but these voters were less open than the electorate in general to the idea that a Democrat would protect them from an attack. On this life and death matter, Democrats simply were not competitive among swing voters in 2004.

HOPE, WITH A CAUTIONARY NOTE

President Bush's relatively narrow victory reflected the advantage of incumbency in a time of war rather than a fundamental shift in the partisan or ideological loyalties of the electorate. There was little change in the public's attitudes toward Mr. Bush or the political parties during the campaign, and gay marriage referenda had no discernible impact on either voter turnout or support for the president. Core supporters of the two major parties voted overwhelmingly for their own party's candidate, and voting patterns in 2004 closely resembled voting patterns in 2000.

These findings should console Democrats who worry that a large, energized Republican base will put Democrats at an electoral disadvantage for years to come. Evidence presented here does not support Republican claims that a "turn out the base" strategy is the path to long-term political dominance. To the contrary, Democrats can take comfort in the success of their own turnout efforts in 2004 and should continue to invest resources into similar efforts in the future, for the evidence suggests they yielded positive results.

However, there is a strong cautionary note for Democrats as well. If Bush did not win the 2004 election on the strength of his core supporters, the small group of swing voters who do not show enduring allegiance to one of the two parties remains critically important to national electoral success. And, among swing voters, Democrats lack credibility on the single issue—national security—which trumped all others in their choice of a candidate. Despite serious misgivings about President Bush's economic policies and his handling of the war in Iraq, swing voters overwhelmingly preferred the Republican Party to the Democratic Party on the issue of who would keep them safe from terrorism.

Given the likelihood that the war on terrorism will remain a major focus of public concern in 2008, these results suggest that in order to regain control of the White House, Democrats will first need to reduce the current overwhelming Republican advantage among swing voters on national security issues.

NOTES

1. John F. Harris, "'04 Voting: Realignment—Or a Tilt?" *Washington Post*, 17 December 2004.

2. Harris, "'04 Voting."

3. Harris, "'04 Voting."

4. Michael P. McDonald, "Up, Up, and Away! Voter Participation in the 2004 Presidential Election," *Forum* 2, no. 4 (2004), available at http://www.bepress.com/forum/vol2/iss4/art4.

5. Alan I. Abramowitz, "An Improved Model for Predicting Presidential Election Outcomes," *PS: Political Science and Politics* 21 (1989): 843–46.

6. The independent variables in this analysis are Bush's percentage of the vote in 2000, a dummy variable for states with gay marriage referenda, a dummy variable for the three states in the New York metropolitan area that were most directly affected by the September 11, 2001, terrorist attacks, and the unemployment rate in the state prior to the election. There is also a term for the estimated turnout of eligible voters in 2004.

7. These results are based on interviews with almost 45,000 registered voters during 2000 and almost 68,000 during 2004.

8. It should be noted, however, that the distribution of party identification in the U.S. electorate has undergone a dramatic change since the 1970s, when Democratic identifiers outnumbered Republican identifiers by a wide margin. See Alan I. Abramowitz and Kyle L. Saunders, "Ideological Realignment in the U.S. Electorate," *Journal of Politics* 60 (1998): 634–52.

9. Abramowitz and Saunders, "Ideological Realignment."

10. The Wald statistics (which are computed by squaring the ratio of each regression coefficient to its standard error) and significance tests indicate that after controlling for party identification, opinions on national security issues had a strong and highly significant influence on the vote, while the effects of New Deal issues and social issues were much weaker and statistically insignificant.

3

MOVING BEYOND THE GENDER GAP

Anna Greenberg

The shrinking of the Democratic margin among women voters was the most important—and perhaps the least noticed—development of the 2004 election. In the two previous presidential campaigns, the Democratic candidate triumphed among women voters by 16 percentage points (Bill Clinton) and 11 points (Al Gore). In contrast, John Kerry won women voters by a mere 3 points, 51 to 48 percent. Not only did the Democratic candidate garner less support among women than in the past, but the overall size of the gender gap narrowed as Bush maintained a solid 11-point margin among men. The small gender gap is consistent with the results of the 2002 congressional elections, when Democrats and Republicans essentially broke even among women, in contrast to 1998 and 2000 when congressional Democrats won women voters by 6 and 8 points, respectively.

This development is not a happy one for progressives, because it signals the chipping away of the foundation that attached women to the Democratic Party. In the past, economic issues helped cement socially conservative, white, blue-collar women to the Democratic Party, while social issues such as support for a woman's right to choose kept more progressive, often college-educated women in the Democratic camp. As Democrats failed to compete on economic issues in the last two election cycles, they lost socially conservative downscale women largely on cultural and security issues. In the absence of an economic alternative, security and morality crowded out the issues where Democrats compete most strongly.

But this did not happen overnight; beginning in 1994, Democrats experienced a drop-off of white, social-conservative women supporters as politics became increasingly polarized around cultural issues. Of course, the growing salience of cultural issues began much earlier—as early as the 1960s when the women's movement and the backlash to societal changes mobilized actors and organizations on the left and the right—but the 1994 elections represent a low moment from which the Democrats have never recovered. The 1996 election with a strong economy, a weak Republican opponent, and a Democratic incumbent with a compelling values narrative was a temporary respite from these trends, but it was just a respite.

To address the issue of women's declining support for the Democratic Party, progressives need to cease thinking of women as a monolithic voting bloc and understand that the differences among them are fundamental and polarizing. Women cannot be approached politically as a unified set of actors with similar interests; rather, they need to be targeted as distinct groups of voters with different political preferences and agendas. Moving forward, progressives need to consider where they can increase support among like-minded women voters, where they can move persuadable women voters to the progressive side of the ledger, and how they can diminish their losses among other women. Specifically, Democrats should consider the distinct voting patterns of the following groups of women:

- *Unmarried women.* Unmarried women are among the most progressive voters in the electorate. They are economic populists who are socially liberal and support Democrats by wide margins. Yet, they underparticipate in politics relative to their married counterparts. In 2004, organizations such as Women's Voices, Women's Vote successfully helped increase their share of the vote in the electorate, but there is considerable room for growth.
- *Older women.* Older women are the quintessential swing voters. They have been splitting their vote nearly evenly between the par-

ties for almost a decade, and their support ebbs and flows depending on how the parties speak to them. In 2004, Kerry lost an opportunity to win older women, which probably cost him the election, by failing to speak to their very serious concerns about their long-term economic security.

- *White, socially conservative women.* Democrats lose white blue-collar women and white married women by large margins; in fact, these women could almost be considered Republican base voters. Yet, there are important openings with these conservative voters. They have concerns about their families that can be addressed by progressives, such as the prevalence of violence and sexual content on television, video games, and the Internet. They are pragmatic and want to protect their children, by making sure they have access to comprehensive sex education in school, and their parents, through stem cell research into chronic medical conditions. Progressives should be able stop the hemorrhage among these women by reframing what it means to care about children and families.

These strategies do not require progressives and Democrats to shift to the center on issues like support for reproductive rights, support for "traditional marriage," or the advancement of women's rights. On the contrary, there is no evidence that shifting to the center will bring in socially conservative women, who understand very well that the Democratic Party supports a woman's right to choose. Instead, Democrats need to offer a strong economic agenda for women that cuts across all of these groups, addressing concerns about health care that are fundamental to unmarried and older women and not an anathema to conservative women. Most importantly, Democrats must reframe the cultural debate, which progressives cannot win in its current incarnation.

THE HISTORY OF THE WOMEN'S VOTE

To understand the decline in the Democratic share of the women's vote, we need to look at the composition of and changes within the women's vote over the past twenty-five years.[1] Traditionally, scholars date the emergence of the gender gap to the 1980 presidential election, when women were less likely than men to support Ronald Reagan's candidacy.[2] In that year, 47 percent of women supported Reagan compared to 55 percent of men, a gap rooted in greater attachment to the welfare state and humanitarian concerns, opposition to militarism, and the rise of women's autonomy through their entry into the labor force and high divorce rates.

While the size of the gender gap varied in the 1980s, it was firmly established by the 1990s in presidential and congressional races. Surveys and exit polls consistently showed that women were more likely than men to vote for Democratic candidates and identify with the Democratic Party. In 1992, for example, 45 percent of women supported Bill Clinton compared to 41 percent of men; the gap grew in 1996, when 54 percent of women supported Clinton's reelection compared to 43 percent of men. Al Gore garnered similar levels of support among women, polling 54 percent compared to only 42 percent among men.

As many scholars note, this persistent gender gap is rooted in the different policy preferences that men and women hold. Women are more progressive than men in their views toward the proper role of government and the scale of social welfare programs. Men support the use of force in international matters and are supportive of defense spending in greater numbers than women.[3] Men are more conservative on racial matters, though women are more conservative about civil liberties, in part because they are less libertarian in their views than men. Women are more progressive on the hot-button social issues of the day such as gay marriage. Thirty-eight percent of women support gay marriage compared to just 22 percent of men.[4] Likewise, 48 percent of women oppose a constitutional amendment to ban gay marriage, compared with only 39 percent of men.[5] As each party has relatively distinctive real or perceived differences on these issues, it is not surprising that women would lean Democratic while men would lean Republican.

The wide margins garnered by Democrats among women in 1996 and 2000 eroded in 2002 and 2004 (see figure 3.1). One of the most prominent explanations for this erosion of support posits that women moved away from Democrats in response to security issues after the September 11, 2001, terrorist attacks. In fact, the decline is actually the result of many years of internal changes in the women's vote. In particular, starting in the mid-1990s, Democrats experienced serious trouble with

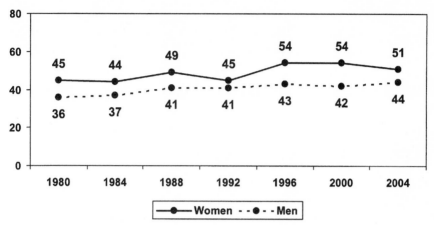

Figure 3.1.   The Gender Gap
Source: Voter News Service Exit Poll and Edison/Mitofsky National Election Pool Exit Poll.
Note: Percentage voting Democratic.

socially conservative, white, blue-collar and married women voters, who began to move over to the Republican Party.

The trend emerged most dramatically in congressional elections (see figure 3.2). Between 1992 and 1994, Democrats lost 10 points among white women without a college education, while actually gaining 3 points with white college-educated women. While Democrats made up

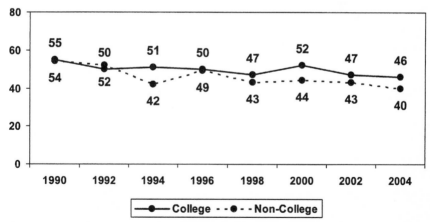

Figure 3.2.   Congressional Vote: White College Women vs. White Non-College Women
Source: Voter News Service Exit Poll and Edison/Mitofsky National Election Pool Exit Poll.
Note: Percentage voting Democratic.

some ground in 1996, when the economy was booming and Clinton easily sailed toward reelection, they lost their standing again in 1998 when
Democrats lost white women without a college education by 11 points.
In 2000 and 2002, Democrats lost white women without a college education by 10 and 12 points, respectively. While Democrats have also experienced some erosion with white college-educated women, that group
remains significantly more Democratic in its voting habits than its blue-
collar counterpart.

The decline in support among white blue-collar women appeared in
presidential elections as well (see figure 3.3). In 2000, Gore lost white
women without a college education by 7 points after Clinton won them
by 7 points in 1996. At the same time, Gore maintained Democratic
standing with white college-educated women. In 2004, these class divisions were firmly entrenched. Bush made gains with all women, but the
increasing softness among blue-collar women took its toll. Kerry lost
white non-college women by 19 points, while losing white college-
educated women by 2 points.

The same pattern of decline among socially conservative white
women is evident among white married women, as figures 3.4 and 3.5
attest. White married women remained competitive for Democrats in
the 1990 and 1992 elections. In 1994, however, Democrats lost white

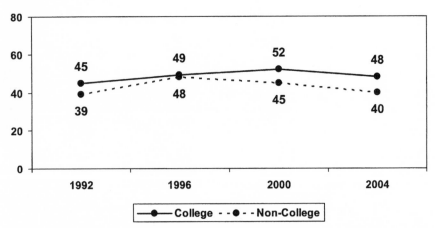

**Figure 3.3.   Presidential Vote: White College Women vs. White Non-College
Women**
Source: Voter News Service Exit Poll and Edison/Mitofsky National Election Pool Exit Poll.
Note: Percentage voting Democratic.

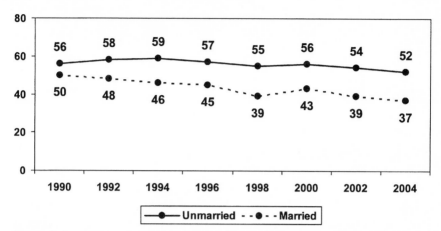

Figure 3.4. Congressional Vote: White Married Women vs. White Unmarried Women
Source: Voter News Service Exit Poll and Edison/Mitofsky National Election Pool Exit Poll.
Note: Percentage voting Democratic.

married women by 6 points and have never regained this lost ground. In every congressional election between 1994 and 2002, Democrats lost white married women by 10 to 19 points; in 2004, that margin increased to 21 points. In presidential elections, the pattern is a little less clear but follows the same trajectory. Democratic presidential candidates lost

Figure 3.5. Presidential Vote: White Married Women vs. White Unmarried Women
Source: Voter News Service Exit Poll and Edison/Mitofsky National Election Pool Exit Poll.
Note: Percentage voting Democratic.

white married women by 3 to 4 points in 1992 and 1996, by 9 points in 2000, and by 23 points in 2004.[6]

WHY WOMEN SHIFTED RIGHT

Clearly, the September 11 attacks and George Bush's standing on the war on terrorism played an important role in the movement of all voters—including women—toward Bush and in solidifying the movement of white, blue-collar, socially conservative women into the Republican camp after the 2000 election. But as these data make clear, the trend among white blue-collar and married women was evident as early as 1994, accelerated in 2000, and was locked in by 2004.

The erosion of support for Democratic candidates among white blue-collar and married women represents a political shift driven by the rise of and polarization around cultural issues in American politics. This transformation story is long and complicated and built upon thirty years of organized "backlash" against the 1960s social movements, particularly around issues of gender, marriage, and sexuality.[7] Suffice it to say that the political parties (in tandem with their allied groups) moved in different directions on many of these issues; while this movement did not necessarily represent a fundamental attitudinal shift among voters (e.g., attitudes about abortion have been remarkably stable since the 1970s), the relative salience of these issues in the electorate increased and were reflected in real and perceived differences between the parties.[8] By the 1980s, Democrats were clearly seen as liberal champions of "rights," while Republicans were seen as conservative defenders of "traditional" values.

Not surprisingly, over time, socially conservative groups moved into the Republican Party, while socially liberal groups solidified their support for the Democratic Party. We see this dynamic most dramatically in the case of white evangelical Christians,[9] but we also see movement among other white socially conservative voters, such as white blue-collar and married voters. Obviously there are many forces producing this shift, and in fact, white men from the South started abandoning the Democratic Party in the late 1950s.[10] But, the most important dynamic to note for this study is that, as the Republican Party successfully de-

fined itself as the party of traditional marriage, white, socially conservative women who saw themselves as defenders of traditional marriage
moved to the Republican camp.[11]

The mid-1990s witnessed an overall collapse of white blue-collar support for the Democratic Party.[12] No doubt Democrats have been com-
plicit in this transformation, as they have alternately abandoned or
struggled with offering an effective populist economic message to blue-
collar voters. As Stanley Greenberg argues in *The Two Americas*, the
"missing middle" as a central narrative for Democrats was all but abandoned by Bill Clinton after the 1994 Congressional defeat.[13] More recently, the decision not to fight the Bush tax cuts to the wealthy in 2001
and the failure to offer an economic message in the 2002 congressional
elections contributed to a disastrous off-year election for the Democrats. And the absence of a real economic narrative coming out of the
Kerry campaign, in an election almost totally focused on security, Iraq,
and cultural issues, undercut Democratic advantages on economic issues during a time of great economic uncertainty.[14]

At the same time, the GOP and its allies spent considerable resources
undermining Democratic advantages on economic issues, which has had
a big impact on women voters. In 2000, when George W. Bush presented himself as a "compassionate conservative" by emphasizing, in
part, education reform, he successfully neutralized Democratic advantages on education policy with suburban women. The $20 million spent
by the pharmaceutical lobby in the 2002 congressional races diminished
Democratic advantages on prescription drugs and retirement issues in
competitive House races. In fact, the top two reasons white blue-collar
women gave for voting Republican in 2002 were to protect Social Security and to reduce the price of prescription drugs.[15]

The post–September 11 political climate and Bush's war on terrorism
locked these gains in place. White blue-collar and married women—like
their white male counterparts—offer high marks to Bush on the war on
terrorism and credit Republicans for keeping them safe. But too much
has been made of the effect of security concerns on the women's vote.
These favorable views by women toward Republicans on safety matters
have been widely cited as the basis for the emergence of the so-called
security mom voter—white married women with children who, as "soc-
cer moms" in the 1990s, had supported Bill Clinton, but who shifted

sharply to Bush during the 2004 campaign because they trusted him to keep their families safe.[16] Analysts, for example, pointed to the terrorist attack in the fall of 2004 on a school in Beslan, Russia, as the moment in the presidential campaign when these women moved into the Republican camp because news of the Russian attack crystallized their fears about their own children's safety.

The problem with this popular analysis is that it is not true. Tracking data dispute the claim of a sudden, permanent shift toward Bush by married women with children, and there is no evidence to suggest that the security mom is much more than a caricature created by the media in an effort to explain the shrinking gender gap at a time when security concerns are a constant presence in the headlines. As the above data make clear, the erosion of support among these women began long before most Americans had ever heard of Osama bin Laden—in the mid-1990s, and certainly not in September 2004.

Equally important, in both 2000 and 2002, white blue-collar and married women voted Republican because they found Bush to be a man of faith—a moral leader—at a time when they were also looking for a dif-

Table 3.1.   Reasons to Vote for Bush in 2004

Reason[a]	Total (%)	White Non-College Women (%)	White Married Women (%)
Response to 9/11 Attack	37	36	37
Terrorism	32	32	30
Decisive Leader	31	25	33
His Religious Faith	29	40	38
Abortion	20	27	26
Tax Cuts	20	13	17
The Iraq War	16	17	14
Economy in Right Direction	15	9	11
Gay Marriage	14	19	16
Made Country Safer	12	12	15
His Education Changes	9	11	12
Gun Owner Rights	9	9	7
Social Security Plans	6	7	5
His Prescription Drug Plan	3	3	3

Source: Democracy Corps/IAF 2004 Post-Election Survey
[a] Percentage, among those who voted or considered voting for Bush, who selected the given reason in response to the question: "Let me read you a list of reasons to (vote/consider voting) for George Bush. Which three best describe the issues and qualities that lead you to (vote/consider voting) for him?"

ferent kind of leadership in the White House. Moreover, white blue-collar and married women saw Bush's decisiveness around 9/11 as an indication of his character and leadership qualities as much as part of a successful effort to make them safer. And they voted Republican because they agreed with Bush on social issues like abortion and to a lesser extent on gay marriage (see table 3.1).

SWINGING WOMEN

Clearly we cannot conceive of a monolithic women's vote; women voters split nearly evenly in the last two elections, and there are huge internal differences among women.[17] Progressives need to think about how to address women voters as discreet blocs, with different interests and agendas that require different persuasion and mobilization strategies. For unmarried women, the goal should be to increase turnout and Democratic margins. For older women, the goal should be to persuade by tapping into economic concerns. And, for white married women, the goal should be to reframe the debate over cultural values to shave off Republican margins.

Unmarried Women

One of the most important societal changes over the past forty years has been the rise of unmarried households. According to *Business Week*, since 1965 we have moved from a country where 80 percent of Americans lived in a household where the head was married to one where only 50 percent do so today.[18] The shift away from "traditional" arrangements to diversity in the choices people make about their lives and families has huge implications for politics and our society as it undergoes this change. There are deep political differences between married and unmarried voters, a "gap" that has been explored in some depth.[19] The chasm between married and unmarried voters is particularly wide among women, and unmarried women are now one of the most progressive and Democratic groups in the electorate.

Unmarried women today are distinct from previous generations. They are better educated, more professional, younger, and more diverse.

Unmarried women in the post–women's movement era are delaying marriage, pursuing careers, getting divorced, and living on their own at levels never seen before. They hold more "feminist" views than their married counterparts, in part because their experiences have pushed them in that direction. At the same time, unmarried women are among the most marginal economic groups in the country, with 54 percent earning less than $30,000 per year (compared to 35 percent in the population overall and 25 percent among married women). They are deeply concerned about their financial security, in particular the availability of affordable health care and, if they are older, their retirement security.

Given this social liberalism and economic marginality, it is not surprising that unmarried women are quite Democratic in their voting behavior. In 2004, unmarried women voted for Kerry by a 25-point margin (see figure 3.6), a performance surpassed by few "base" Democratic groups. Kerry also performed particularly well among white unmarried women (55 to 44 percent), even though white women overall supported President Bush by an 11-point margin (55 to 44 percent). In fact, white unmarried women were the only group of white, low-income women to remain solid in their support for Kerry.

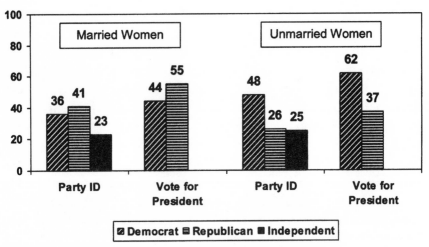

Figure 3.6.   2004 Vote among Key Women's Groups
Source: Edison/Mitofsky National Election Pool Exit Poll.
Note: Percentage responding

Clearly, there is room to increase the share of unmarried women in the electorate. Unmarried women are less likely to be registered and less likely to vote than married women, in part because they are less educated, more mobile, and socially disconnected. Systematic efforts to reach out to unmarried women in 2004 produced an increase in their percent share of the electorate from 19 to 22.4, but this number can be improved.[20] Unmarried women are still underrepresented in the electorate relative to their share of the population.

There may also be room to improve Democratic margins among unmarried women. Just as Karl Rove and the GOP were successful in increasing their margins among white evangelical Christian voters over the past two election cycles, progressives and Democrats have much to offer unmarried women. Unmarried women are particularly hurt by the GOP's economic and social agenda. They were among the least likely to benefit from the Bush tax cuts and they will be left behind on healthcare policy—their number one concern—through cuts to Medicaid in state budgets. They are significantly to the left of the Republican Party on social issues ranging from a woman's right to choose to Title IX gender equity issues, and they understand that they are the targets of the Bush administration's "marriage initiatives." Their number one priority after access to affordable health care is pay equity and retirement security.[21] Progressives and Democrats can easily address these issues.

Older Women

While unmarried women are close to becoming a base Democratic group, older women remain a swing group. Like unmarried women, older women represent a sizeable chunk of voters—27 percent—and will be even larger as the Baby Boomers age.[22] They are "cross-pressured" by significant economic concerns surrounding health care and retirement security that conflict with socially conservative views, particularly if they are white and blue collar. Figure 3.7 shows the considerable variability in the voting patterns of older women in the last four presidential election cycles, with their Democratic share of the vote ranging from 47 to 55 percent.

In 2004, Kerry won older women by 3 points, 51 to 48 percent, but lost older white women by 5 points—a 4-point drop in support for the

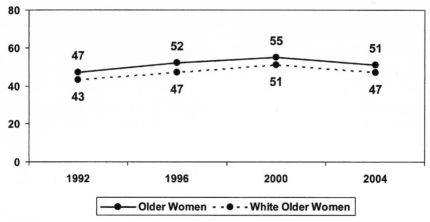

Figure 3.7.   Presidential Vote: Older Women vs. White Older Women
Source: Voter News Service Exit Poll and Edison/Mitofsky National Election Pool Exit Poll.
Note: Percentage voting Democratic

Democratic candidate since 2000. In fact, Bush posted the best performance by a Republican among older women since 1988. Still, Kerry
had the opportunity to maintain and perhaps increase Democratic support among older women. In early 2004, campaign advertising in the
battleground states emphasized health care and domestic priorities.[23]
During this period (February to April), Kerry held a lead among white
older women by an average of 7 points, 49 to 42 percent, and among
white older non-college women by 2 points, 46 to 44 points. On Election Day, following a campaign steeped in values and security discussion
rather than economic matters, Kerry lost white older women by 5
points, 47 to 52 percent, and white older non-college women by 18
points, 40 to 58 percent. Even more striking, there was a 14-point gap
among white, older, non-college women between their identification
with the Democratic Party (a 4-point Democratic disadvantage) and
their support for Kerry (an 18-point disadvantage).[24]

Kerry lost ground with older white women when the national discussion moved from health care, retirement, and other domestic priorities
to security, the war on terrorism, and conduct of the war in Iraq. Kerry
himself facilitated this shift by staging a Democratic Convention focused on security and military experience, after which economic issues
were largely absent from the national debate. The changing agenda sig-

nificantly hurt Kerry's chances with cross-pressured older women voters, who were inclined to support Bush on security and "moral values." Time series data show that support for Kerry dropped precipitously among older white women by September (as it did with all voters), and it never really returned among these voters even as he improved nationally. In the absence of a real economic discussion, these voters swung to Bush as he tapped into their social conservatism, their support for his approach to the war on terrorism, and their admiration of his religious faith.

There is an important lesson to learn from 2004: when we fail to address their issues, we lose older women voters to cultural conservatism. Even in a campaign whose broad themes are about security, it is possible to target older women voters with messages that address their economic concerns, as Kerry did with his early battleground-state advertising. Unlike younger, socially conservative women, older women *want* to vote their economic security. Democrats need to give them that option. As we are in the midst of an important discussion about Social Security reform, progressives have an outstanding opportunity to stake out ground as the champions of long-term financial security. Doing so will yield critically important support among this key group of swing voters.

MOVING BEYOND THE "SECURITY MOM"

Despite the lively media debate about the fabled "security mom," younger white married women with kids have been moving away from Democratic candidates for years, and 2004 simply represented the culmination of this departure. Kerry fared badly with this group, losing white married women by 23 points, 61 to 38 percent, and white married women with kids by 31 points, 65 to 34 percent (see figure 3.8). Like unmarried women, these white, socially conservative women voters are essentially GOP base voters.

It is unrealistic to believe that Democrats can make major gains with this group, even if our national political discussion moves away from security issues. Their attachment to the Republican Party is based on a wide range of cultural concerns that encompasses far more than just security. Their support has been cultivated over many years by Republicans

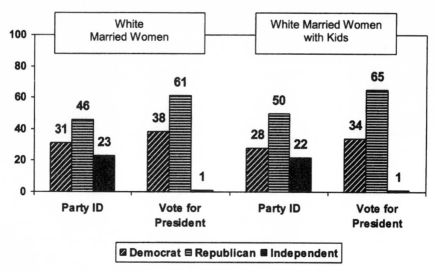

Figure 3.8.   2004 Vote: White Married Women vs. White Married Women with Kids
Source: Edison/Mitofsky National Election Pool Exit Poll.
Note: Percentage responding

through highly effective organized activity by conservative groups such as Concerned Women for America and Focus on the Family. Moreover, economic concerns are simply not as salient to younger white married women as they are to older and unmarried women, and they are likely to have benefited from Bush's tax policies such as the child tax credit and the elimination of the marriage penalty. Unlike older women, Democrats cannot win this group just through an appeal to alternative economic policies.

But white married women with kids have a range of concerns that are perfectly appropriate for progressives and Democrats to address. Reaching them requires reframing the cultural debate and expanding it to include a host of issues that concern their ability to raise children in a safe and healthy environment. Rather than accept the Right's narrow definition of values (i.e., abortion, gay marriage), progressives should acknowledge the challenges parents face dealing with their kids' sexuality and peer pressure around drugs and alcohol in an environment overrun with sex and violence on television, the Internet, and video games. Democrats and progressives should begin to talk about these concerns in simple language and should not shy away from taking progressive positions that are consistent with what moms value.

Moms are pragmatic and want their children to be raised with the right kind of values that will allow them to make responsible choices about their behavior. They want their kids to be faithful, be responsible, and understand the "Golden Rule," and they worry that their kids will be sexually active too soon or will be exposed to alcohol and drugs. These concerns are neither inherently liberal nor conservative; many progressives share them and would be wise to engage in a discussion of these values. In this context, progressives can trumpet positions on social issues that are more in step with these voters' concerns than positions taken by the Republican Party. The vast majority of moms support sex education in public schools and access to birth control, which the Bush administration and its allies oppose through their advocacy of "abstinence only" education. Moms support stem cell research and worry about the impact of pollution on their children's health and safety, areas where the GOP has staked out entirely different ground.[25]

Democrats and progressives, therefore, have an opportunity to reframe the cultural debate by emphasizing the ways that they care about families rather than by fighting defensive battles that box them into the "antifamily" corner. We do not have to retreat from supporting values we hold most dearly—like protecting a woman's right to choose or only supporting "traditional" marriage—because, as John Kenneth White argues in this book, cultural arguments need not have a left–right dimension or be policy specific. Democrats will be successful with women voters if they cast progressive responses to cultural issues in the same commonsense language moms use when they express concerns about their children. Even better, progressives do have policy positions consistent with these concerns.

Progressives can only make gains in cultural battles by taking the offensive in places where we can and should win. At the same time, we need to be realistic: we cannot make major gains with white conservative women in the short run. However, we can make inroads, diminishing the advantage Republicans hold with a core constituency and laying the foundation for a future when we seriously contest, rather than lose, values battles.

WINNING BACK WOMEN

For Democrats and progressives, debate about the women's vote needs to move beyond whether or not the gender gap shrank in 2004. It needs to put aside narrow arguments about misleading concerns about women and security. Progressives and Democrats instead need to acknowledge that there is a problem with the "women's vote" and focus on how to re-build support among white blue-collar and married women, regain ground with older women, and increase the participation of women who support a progressive political agenda. This task can be accomplished by putting aside talk of a monolithic "women's vote" and thinking about women voters as large, discreet groups with their own agendas. Each group plays a distinct strategic role in building a progressive majority, and each needs to be approached with a distinct set of tactics. But this does *not* mean that communicating with women should be a narrow or particularistic project. In fact, Democrats and progressives fare badly with women when they do not have a broad economic and cultural nar-rative that informs who they are as a party or a movement.

Moreover, an effective strategy for reaching out to women voters, par-ticularly married women with children, necessitates going on the offen-sive in cultural battles where Democrats and progressives have been forced into a defensive position. Because of the positions held by mar-ried women, this can be done without sacrificing core progressive ideals. It is time for progressives to take the initiative and offer a clear, com-monsense economic vision while reframing the "values" debate to ad-dress the concrete concerns women have about raising their families in a society that often seems to be operating in a different reality than their own. These two foci cut across the concerns of all women voters and are the building blocks for bringing women into a successful progressive electoral coalition.

NOTES

1. Most of the data in this chapter come from the VNS exit polls and the Edison/Mitofsky National Election Pool. Voter News Service (VNS) was founded in 1993 as a consortium owned by ABC, AP, NBC, CBS, CNN, and

Fox to provide conclusive, accurate, and efficient exit polling for major elections. To deal with the problems in the VNS system in 2000 and 2002, ABC, AP, NBC, CBS, CNN, and Fox created the National Election Pool to provide tabulated vote counts and exit poll surveys for the major 2004 presidential primaries and the November general election. These six major news organizations used Edison Media Research and Mitofsky International as the provider of exit polls. Nationally, they interviewed 13,660 respondents on Election Day.

2. As many argue, the gender gap that emerged between men and women was as much a product of the flight of men from the Democratic Party as it was a result of the influx of women into the party. See Laura R. Winsky-Mattei and Franco Mattei, "If Men Stayed at Home . . . The Gender Gap in Recent Congressional Elections," *Political Research Quarterly* 51, no. 2 (June 1998): 411–36.

3. A poll of 2,186 adults by the Pew Research Center for the People and the Press from April 24–May 6, 2000, shows a wide gender gap on support for developing a missile defense system. Forty-five percent of men supported developing this capacity even if it alienates Russia, compared to 27 percent of women.

4. A National Public Radio survey conducted by Greenberg Quinlan Rosner Research and Public Opinion Strategies surveyed 1,002 likely voters on this issue between December 10 and 15, 2003. The survey has a margin of error of ±3.1 percent. It is available at http://www.npr.org/templates/story/story.php?storyId=4512392.

5. According to the University of Pennsylvania's National Annenberg Election Survey, conducted June 5–8, 2004, and released June 10, 2004. The survey includes 1,230 registered voters and has a margin of error of ±3 percent. The one exception is "women's issues" such as abortion, where the differences between men and women are relatively small. That said, there is no doubt that for certain women on both sides of the debate, abortion motivates political decision making.

6. The Perot vote obscures these margins to a degree. In 1992, research shows that the Perot vote would have split evenly between Clinton and Bush, suggesting that the margin between white unmarried and married women would have remained the same. In 1996, the Perot vote was heavily Republican; had Perot not been on the ticket, Dole would have performed significantly better with white married women.

7. For particularly strong accounts of this history, see Jane J. Mansbridge, *Why We Lost the ERA* (Chicago: University of Chicago Press, 1986); and Donald G. Matthews and Jane Sherron De Hart, *Sex, Gender and the Politics of the ERA* (New York: Oxford University Press, 1990).

8. Edward G. Carmines and Geoffrey C. Layman, "Issue Evolution in Postwar American Politics: Old Certainties and Fresh Tensions," in *Present Discontents*, ed. B. E. Shafer (Chatham, N.J.: Chatham House Publishers, 1997); Christina Wollbrecht, *The Politics of Women's Rights* (Princeton, N.J.: Princeton University Press, 2000).

9. Kenneth D. Wald, *Religion and Politics in the United States*, 3rd ed. (Washington, D.C.: Congressional Quarterly Press, 1997).

10. Anna Greenberg, "Why Men Leave: Gender and Partisanship in the 1990s," paper presented at the annual meeting of the American Political Science Association, Washington, D.C., August 31–September 3, 2000.

11. Kristen Luker, *Abortion and the Politics of Motherhood* (Berkeley: University of California Press, 1984).

12. Ruy Teixeira and Joel Rogers, *America's Forgotten Majority* (New York: Basic Books, 2000).

13. Stanley B. Greenberg, *The Two Americas* (New York: Thomas Dunne Books, 2004).

14. Stanley B. Greenberg and James Carville, "Solving the Paradox of 2004: Why America Wanted Change but Voted for Continuity," Democracy Corps, November 9, 2004, available at http://www.greenbergresearch.com/publications/dcorps/11052004_Post_Election_2004_solving_the_paradox.pdf.

15. Anna Greenberg, "Where Were the Women?" *Nation* 275, no. 23 (December 30, 2002): 20.

16. Anna Greenberg, "The Security Mom Myth—Updated," Greenberg Quinlan Rosner Research, September 28, 2004, available at http://www.greenbergresearch.com/publications/reports/r_security_mom_myth092804.pdf.

17. Anna Greenberg, "Race, Religiosity, and the Women's Vote," *Women and Politics* 22, no. 3 (2001): 59–82.

18. Michelle Conlin, "UnMarried America," *Business Week*, October 20, 2003, 106.

19. Anna Greenberg, "The Marriage Gap," *Blueprint* 11 (July 12, 2001), available at http://www.ndol.org/ndol_ci.cfm?kaid=114&subid=144&contentid=3559.

20. Women's Voices, Women's Vote was a national effort designed to increase the registration and turnout of unmarried women. For information, see http://www.wvwv.org.

21. Anna Greenberg and Jennifer Berktold, "Unmarried Women in the 2004 Presidential Election," Greenberg Quinlan Rosner Research, January 2005, available at http://www.greenbergresearch.com/publications/reports/wvwv_postelection.pdf.

22. Here, we define older as more than 50 years of age.

23. During this period, the Kerry campaign, MoveOn.Org, the Media Fund, and the AFL-CIO and other unions were airing ads in the battleground states. Most of these ads addressed economic issues such as jobs, healthcare costs, and retirement security.

24. Democracy Corps/Institute for America's Future, "Democracy Corps/Institute for America's Future Post-Election Survey Frequency Questionnaire," November 2–3, 2004, available at http://www.greenbergresearch .com/publications/dcorps/dsurvey/11052004_Post_Election_Survey_November_ 2-3_2004.pdf.

25. Two surveys conducted by Greenberg Quinlan Rosner Research and commissioned by Club Mom in 2004 and 2005 demonstrate support by mothers for stem cell research and comprehensive sex educational programs. The 2004 study surveyed 1,207 mothers nationally between March 8 and 11, 2004, with over-samples of 139 African-American mothers and 121 Hispanic mothers; it has a margin of error of ±2.82 percent. The 2005 study surveyed 1,003 mothers nationally between February 17 and 21, 2005, and has a margin of error of ±3.1 percent.

4

SOLVING THE VALUES DILEMMA

John Kenneth White

In May 1997, Bill Clinton had much to smile about. Seven months removed from an easy reelection victory, Clinton was triumphantly thinking ahead to the presidential election three years hence. Meeting with his closest advisors, he outlined his political strategy: "Strategically, I want to remove all divisive issues for a conservative candidate, so all the issues are on progressive terrain." To that end, Clinton and his staff worked on a speech outlining plans for his remaining thousand days in office. After copies of the address were circulated, Al Gore took aim at the speechwriters: "One word that doesn't jump at me in these documents is 'values.' And if you were in a room full of Republicans doing the same thing, that would be number one on their list."[1]

Clinton immediately grasped Gore's point. For years, he had studied how Republican politicians—especially Ronald Reagan—had been able to forge a values connection with voters by preaching the virtues of "family, work, neighborhood, peace, and freedom."[2] Several subliminal values buttressed Reagan's message, including self-esteem, patriotism, self-realization, and religiosity. More than a listing of mere platitudes, Reagan's litany enabled him to structure political discourse, as his pollster Richard Wirthlin explained:

> In being the person who establishes a tone, a president has influence on every American be it a young person entering the job market, an individual

on the margin of deciding whether to study or whether to work, or an entrepreneur trying to determine whether to invest in his own business or go to work for someone else.[3]

From the start of his administration to its denouement, Ronald Reagan cloaked nearly all of his speeches in values talk. For example, while bidding farewell to the delegates at the 1988 Republican National Convention, Reagan told of a letter he received from a young boy that read, in part: "I love America because you can join the Cub Scouts if you want to. You have a right to worship as you please. If you have the ability, you can try to be anything you want to be."[4]

Despite the power of Reagan's words, the Republican Party suffered from a values deficit during the 1980s. An examination of the handful of poll questions asked prior to 1988 shows that it was the *Democrats* who had a strong advantage when asked which party better protected traditional family values (see table 4.1). Thus, Reagan's values strategy resulted in political successes that accrued to him, not his party.

In 1988, George H. W. Bush figured out how to succeed where Reagan did not. Seeking the presidency, Bush used values to attack his opponent, painting Democratic rival Michael S. Dukakis as an unworthy values steward. This strategy crystallized when the Bush campaign in-

Table 4.1.   Democratic Party Values Advantage, 1974–1986

Question	Democrats (%)	Republicans (%)
When it comes right down to it, do you feel that the Democratic Party or the Republican Party more closely represents your views and values, or don't you feel either one really does? (1974)[a]	47	15
Is the Republican or the Democratic Party the party of traditional family values? (1984)[b]	40	29
Regardless of how you usually vote, do you think the Republican Party or the Democratic Party is the party of traditional family values? (1986)[c]	45	33

[a]Yankelovich, Skelly and White, March 1974
[b]CBS News/New York Times, August 5–9, 1984
[c]CBS News/New York Times, September 28–October 1, 1986

vited two dozen residents from Paramus, New Jersey, to a local hotel to talk about the candidates. Most of these blue-collar Roman Catholics had previously backed Reagan but were now leaning to Dukakis. All that changed when the moderator asked, "What if I told you that Dukakis vetoed a bill that required school children to say the Pledge of Allegiance? Or that he was against the death penalty? Or that he gave weekend furloughs to first-degree murderers?" Their responses were loud and clear: "He's a liberal!" said one participant. "If those are really his positions," said another, "I'd have a hard time supporting him."[5] Historian Garry Wills wrote: "It was a brilliant stroke to run the incumbent Vice-President, who was boasting of his own Administration's success, as the candidate of *grievance*—of affronts localized in a liberalism that is soft on crime and defense, exotic as a Harvard boutique, yet stealthy enough to win an election by misrepresenting itself to the American people."[6]

FROM BOOM TO BUST: BILL CLINTON, FAMILY VALUES, AND THE DEMOCRATIC PARTY

Bill Clinton inherited a dispirited Democratic Party in 1992, but he turned things around by skillfully adapting Reagan-era values phrases as his own. Clinton understood the power of values rhetoric, often making frequent references to "opportunity, community, and responsibility" in his speeches. For example, upon accepting the Democratic nomination, he declared: "We offer our people a new choice based on old values. We offer opportunity. And we demand responsibility. The choice we offer is not conservative or liberal, Democratic or Republican. It is different. It is new. And it will work."[7] Even in his farewell address, Clinton was still speaking about values: "I have steered my course by our enduring values: opportunity for all, responsibility from all, a community of all Americans."[8] In sum, *opportunity, community, and responsibility* was a mantra that Clinton employed over and over again.

Initially, Clinton's values talk paid off. In 1992, 51 percent of Americans said that when Clinton spoke about family values he was referring to their own families.[9] Another survey taken that same year found 54 percent believed that the Democratic presidential nominee shared the moral values most Americans try to live by.[10] Accordingly, the Democratic

Party regained its values footing: 34 percent said Democrats did a better job of "upholding traditional family values," a 2-percentage-point advantage over Republicans.[11]

But Clinton's initial years as president were marred by a series of policy decisions that damaged his position with the voters and underscored the long-term values weaknesses of the Democratic Party. The "don't ask, don't tell" fiasco surrounding gays in the military; a failed healthcare proposal put forward by his wife, Hillary; and Clinton's signature on the Brady gun control bill gave Republicans an opening to exploit the negative symbolism associated with these measures. "God, guns, and gays" became the Republican rallying cry—an indictment of how Clinton's actions had *undermined* his stated values of opportunity, community, and responsibility. The GOP charge helped the party to win control of both houses of Congress in 1994 for the first time in forty years.

The 1995 Oklahoma City bombing gave Clinton a second chance to reconnect with voters. Shortly after the tragedy, Clinton's press secretary Michael McCurry observed: "The debate in America is shifting out of economic policy and to moral values and what kind of society we are. The Republicans have had strong, resonant statements on that and the Democrats have fallen short. This [bombing] gives Clinton an opportunity to talk about civil discourse and social values."[12]

Clinton had already begun talking about values again, using his bully pulpit to become the nation's storyteller-in-chief. In his 1995 State of the Union address, which took place prior to the Oklahoma City bombing, Clinton told several stories with a values theme. He spoke of Lynn Woolsey, a single mother who found her way off welfare to become a member of Congress; of Cindy Perry, a mother of four who passed her high school equivalency exam and taught reading to second-graders in rural Kentucky; and of Steven Bishop, the police chief of Kansas City, Missouri, an AmeriCorps volunteer, and an innovator in community policing. He told of Corporal Gregory Depestre, a Haitian-American who was part of the U.S. force that landed in Haiti; praised the Reverends John and Diana Cherry for founding a church in the high-crime and drug-infested neighborhoods of Washington, D.C.; and recognized Jack Lucas, a World War II veteran from Hattiesburg, Mississippi, who was badly wounded at Iwo Jima while saving the lives of three fellow soldiers. Clinton connected the dots between these stories and the values of what he called the New Covenant:

> [This is] at the heart of this New Covenant: responsibility, opportunity, and citizenship. More than stale chapters in some remote civics book they are still the virtues by which we can fulfill ourselves and reach our God-given potential and be like them, and also to fulfill the eternal promise of this country, the enduring dream from that first and most sacred covenant. I believe every person in this country still believes that we are created equal, and given by our Creator the right to life, liberty, and the pursuit of happiness.[13]

In 1996, Clinton never ceded his values rhetoric to his Republican opponent. In an incisive memo, pollsters Mark Penn and Doug Schoen explained how the president could link his opportunity, community, and responsibility mantra to a second-term agenda:

1. *Standing up for America.* Every time our actions and words are interpreted as standing up for America, our support grows. . . . This is not a value we say we are doing, it is one that comes through a series of strong, definite actions that have us standing up to threats in the world from a very U.S. point of view.
2. *Providing opportunities for all Americans.* This is clearly what our defense and expansion of education are all about—giving people the opportunity to make the best of their own lives. Despite all the frustration with government, people are NOT frustrated with their own abilities as long as they and their children are given a chance to get ahead.
3. *Doing what's right even when it is unpopular.* Standing up to the tobacco companies and supporting the assault weapons ban are examples not just of doing what's right, but doing it despite what are perceived as heavy political costs. There is no benefit to a values-based strategy if people say the president is taking the easy way out. Only when they see a cost can they come to admire the actions as extraordinary.
4. *Preserving and promoting families* (helping parents protect kids from the bad in society). In every poll we have taken, this is the top-scoring issue. It is made doubly important by the fact that we are so far behind with the votes of people with families. We have to change the perception

we have of promoting the single-parent family over the conventional,
two-parent family by grouping as many of our programs [as possible]
under a banner of "putting families first."[14]

Clinton listened, and the result was a reversal of his own misfortunes
and those of his party. As Election Day approached, Clinton had a slender but notable 3-percentage-point lead over Bob Dole as the man best
able to deal with the country's moral problems.[15] The Democratic
Party's standing on moral and values issues also improved. When it came
to deciding which party would do the better job of enhancing fairness,
community, and hope, Democrats bested Republicans by 16 points, 13
points, and 10 points, respectively. Only when asked which party did the
better job of promoting personal responsibility did the GOP have a decisive 10-point advantage.[16]

But Bill Clinton and the Democratic Party suffered considerable
damage following the Monica Lewinsky scandal. The injury to Clinton's
personal reputation was made vividly clear when Democratic pollster
Peter D. Hart asked: "Which of the following people, if any, do you
think most symbolizes what is wrong with the country's moral values:
Bill Clinton, Jerry Springer, Linda Tripp, Larry Flynt, Mike Tyson, or
Heidi Fleiss?" Clinton "won" with 30 percent, followed by Springer, 27
percent; Tripp, 12 percent; Flynt, 9 percent; Tyson, 8 percent; and
Fleiss, 2 percent.[17] Linking Clinton to a controversial talk show host, a

Table 4.2.   Democratic Party Values Disadvantage, 1998–1999

Value	Democrats Preferred (%)	Republicans Preferred (%)
Encouraging high moral standards and values (1998)[a]	32	50
Upholding traditional family values (1999)[b]	30	49
Promoting morality and personal responsibility (1998)[c]	27	45
Has the best ideas for improving morality in the country (1999)[d]	29	37
Shares your values (1998)[e]	35	40
Knowing right from wrong (1999)[e]	28	35
Associate with the term "discipline" (1999)[e]	16	49

[a]ABC News/Washington Post, September 25–28, 1998
[b]CBS News/New York Times, November 4–7, 1999
[c]Princeton Survey Research Associates, August 27–September 8, 1998
[d]Pew Research Center, January 1999
[e]Greenberg Quinlan Research, November 29–December 1, 1999

former Lewinsky confidant who tape-recorded her telephone conversations, a pornographer, a disgraced boxer, and a Hollywood madam spoke volumes about the hurt Clinton had inflicted on himself. More troubling was the fact that Clinton's lack of credibility on values issues had undermined his fellow Democrats. Republicans had sizeable leads on a host of values concerns, ranging from protecting traditional family values to being the party that knows the difference between right and wrong. Only when asked which party showed compassion toward the disadvantaged did the Democrats maintain their historic New Deal–era advantage (see table 4.2).

POST-CLINTON: THE DEMOCRATS' VALUES DEFICIT DEEPENS

In the summer of 2000, political analysts Anna Greenberg and Stanley B. Greenberg wrote that after two Clinton terms, Democrats had lost ground in the battle over values:

> People respect the Democrats for their openness to new ideas, their commitment to community, and their defense of tolerance and individual rights. But . . . voters are more impressed with the Republicans' insistence on personal responsibility, discipline, and teaching children about right and wrong. Voters want young people to learn norms and limits. And Democrats are more commonly seen to be permissive about such things.[18]

Not surprisingly, 60 percent told poll-takers that having someone who "shares your moral values" would be a very important factor in making their decision in the upcoming Bush–Gore contest.[19] The public's hunger for values became so paramount that one-quarter of the electorate were reclassified as "values voters."[20]

Al Gore understood this. His choice of Joseph Lieberman as the Democratic party's vice presidential candidate sent a powerful values message, as Lieberman was a devout Orthodox Jew who refused to campaign on Saturdays. Gore also promoted himself as a worthy steward of traditional family values. At the Democratic Convention, he heaped attention on his own family by having his daughter Karenna nominate him for president, and when he took to the stage he embraced his wife, Tipper, and gave her a long, passionate kiss.

The public reacted favorably. By a margin of 49 percent to 41 percent, Americans said the Gore–Lieberman ticket made them feel that the Democratic nominee was a man of faith and strong moral values.[21] Likewise, nearly three-quarters said Gore had high moral and ethical standards, and 58 percent thought he would do a better job than Clinton in providing moral leadership.[22] An ABC News/*Washington Post* poll found Gore and Bush tied at 44 percent apiece when respondents were asked which one would encourage high moral standards and values.[23] This proved to be a harbinger of the electoral deadlock that was to come.

Despite gaining in the polls, Gore was severely disadvantaged by the Democratic Party's poor positioning on values issues. Republicans held a 23-point advantage as the party that better upholds traditional family values; a 15-point edge as the party more closely associated with the value of knowing right from wrong; and a 9-point lead as the party that protects religious values.[24] But it was a poll conducted by NBC News and the *Wall Street Journal* that found the most startling discrepancy between the two parties. When asked whether Republicans stood for strong moral values, 66 percent said yes and only 25 percent answered no. But when the same question was posed about Democrats, voters were evenly divided: 44 percent said yes and 46 percent said no.[25] Although Democrats held an overwhelming 31-point advantage on the question of which party best preserved the value of tolerance, even this positive result could be construed as problematic, as some voters equate tolerance with a libertine lifestyle.[26]

Things did not improve for the Democrats in 2002. The midterm election results revealed a Democratic Party values deficit that severely hurt the party's prospects. Election Day exit polls conducted in ten states by Zogby International found large Republican leads when people were asked which party best promoted hard work, family values, and integrity, while Democrats maintained an advantage only on the questionable issue of tolerance (see table 4.3).

In 2004, things went from bad to worse. The Democratic Party was united and George W. Bush faced anemic job approval ratings (usually in the mid-to-high 40 percent range), a majority of respondents believing that the nation was headed in the wrong direction, and a plurality say-

Table 4.3. Republican Party Values Advantage, 2002

Which political party is better equipped to preserve traditional family values such as

State	Hard Work		Tolerance		Family Values		Integrity	
	Rep (%)	Dem (%)	Rep (%)	Dem (%)	Rep (%)	Dem (%)	Rep (%)	Dem (%)
California	41	33	32	47	39	32	39	31
Iowa	35	38	30	46	40	34	38	32
Michigan	42	35	40	51	43	31	42	25
S. Dakota	42	30	30	39	47	26	47	24
Arkansas	41	38	33	46	40	34	41	34
Minnesota	40	37	29	50	41	32	40	32
Colorado	49	25	27	52	49	28	44	25
New Hampshire	47	23	31	44	44	24	42	22
Georgia	52	29	38	46	53	28	51	28
North Carolina	47	31	34	50	49	28	46	25

Source: Zogby International exit polls, November 5, 2002

ing they were inclined not to reelect him. Historically, these measures have forecast trouble for incumbent presidents. But not this time. While many, including Alan Abramowitz in this volume, legitimately point to national security matters (primarily the terrorist attacks of September 11, 2001, and the war in Iraq) as reasons for Bush's narrow victory, the Democratic Party's continued lack of attention to its values problems—and the consequences resulting from this negligence—are clear.

Democrats seemed to understand the problem. In 2004, John Kerry tried to sell his values story to voters. It largely consisted of his heroic Vietnam War service, culminating in his opening line at the Democratic Convention, "I'm John Kerry, and I'm reporting for duty."[27] Kerry inevitably contrasted his 1960s Vietnam-era experiences with those of George W. Bush, who had an infamously spotty record in the Texas Air National Guard. Kerry caught an early break when a Republican and retired Los Angeles County sheriff named Jim Rassman came forward just before the Iowa caucuses and claimed that the Democratic candidate had rescued him from near-death in Vietnam. Rassman described Kerry's "bravery and leadership under fire" and declared that he would be "a great commander-in-chief."[28] In many ways, the Kerry story contained the echoes of another Democratic icon from Massachusetts, John F. Kennedy, who never tired of telling his story of heroism during World War II on PT-109.

Whenever John Kerry was able to connect his military service to public values (including patriotism, service, and building community), his support rose. For example, starting with a mere 15 percent of the vote in Iowa on January 10, Kerry's support increased to 25 percent eight days later, and he wound up being an easy first-place caucus winner.[29] Sensing danger, the Bush campaign subsequently undermined Kerry's credibility by questioning his Vietnam service. One cannot overstate the detrimental effect on Kerry's electoral performance of the advertisements created by a pseudo-Republican organization called "Swift Boat Veterans for Truth," and the Kerry campaign's slow response to them. To be sure, John Kerry was not a perfect candidate. But these commercials were effective because they were cast against the backdrop of a continued Democratic Party values deficit. For example, a 2004 poll found 42 percent of Americans saying the Republican Party would do a better job of promoting strong moral values; only 21 percent chose the Democrats.[30] Numbers like these helped seal Kerry's fate. On Election Day, 22 percent of voters cited moral values as a primary concern, and 80 percent of them backed George W. Bush.[31]

Clearly, the Democrats do not just have a messenger problem. When it comes to values, they have a *party problem.* Al Gore and John Kerry were on balance effective values messengers. But voters do not see presidential candidates as "lone rangers." In an era marked by intense partisanship, Americans view presidential candidates within the context of their party affiliations. Thus, Democratic nominees are seen as better than Republicans at promoting equality of opportunity, tolerance, and compassion for the little guy, but are regarded as poor defenders of hard work, integrity, and traditional families (see table 4.4). In contrast, Re-

Table 4.4. Democratic Party Values Strengths, 2004

Value	Democratic Strength (%)	Republican Strength (%)
Ensuring equal opportunities	37	10
Tolerance	27	6
Individuality	19	9
Compassion	14	6

Source: NBC News/Wall Street Journal, December 9–13, 2004
Note: Percentages reflect respondent opinion on which values most strongly represent each party.

Table 4.5. Republican Party Values Strengths, 2004

Value	Republican Strength (%)	Democratic Strength (%)
Strengthening Families	31	11
Strong Faith	25	5
Personal Responsibility	21	8
Raising Standards of Public Decency	18	6

Source: NBC News/Wall Street Journal, December 9–13, 2004
Note: Percentages reflect respondent opinion on which values most strongly represent each party.

publican presidential candidates are often viewed as pro-family, having a strong faith, advocating personal responsibility, and raising standards of public decency, and they are often given the benefit of the doubt on these issues, but they are viewed as less tolerant and compassionate than Democrats (see table 4.5).

Each party, then, has to compensate for its weaknesses. George W. Bush was particularly effective in doing so when in 2000 he introduced himself to the voters as a "compassionate conservative," suggesting that he was a different kind of Republican from mean-spirited types like House Speaker Newt Gingrich who had spearheaded the Clinton impeachment drive. Democrats would be wise to take notice of how Bush positioned himself to overcome negative values associated with his party, as they have been less effective than Republicans at compensating for their values weaknesses. More than nominating a candidate for president who is attentive to values, Democrats need to make a high-level institutional commitment to correcting their values weaknesses.

WHAT TO DO?

Democrats have sensed their values weakness, but since the Clinton years they have been unsure how to address it. At times, Democrats have unintentionally hurt their own cause. John Kerry's infamous line about the supplemental budget for the Iraq War—"I actually did vote for the $87 billion before I voted against it"—permitted Bush to label Kerry a "flip-flopper."[32] The moniker stuck because of the preexisting impression that Democrats lack a values anchor. A focus group conducted by Democracy Corps, headed by Democratic strategists James

Carville, Stanley Greenberg, and Bob Shrum, illustrated Kerry's dilemma. One participant noted, "Kerry one day was over here, and then he was over there." Another added, "He's the guy that holds up the line at McDonalds." To Carville and Greenberg, such statements were a devastating indictment of both Kerry and his party: "The collective impression is that Democrats have no strength of conviction or clarity of direction. That reflects the most immediate national election, but also 2002, when Democrats sought the lowest common denominator and failed to challenge the Republicans on taxes, the economy, or Iraq."[33]

While Republicans will always be conservatives in that they espouse freedom and individualism, Democrats must be progressives—especially in trumpeting equality of opportunity, community, and tolerance tempered by responsibility. Today, Republicans enjoy a 28-point advantage over the Democrats as the party that "knows what they stand for."[34] Top-level Democrats instinctively know they must do better. A Gallup survey of Democratic National Committee members conducted prior to the selection of Howard Dean as party chair found 68 percent agreed with the statement that their party should "mainly try to defeat the Republican agenda to draw clear distinctions between the two parties"; only 24 percent said the party should "mainly try to find areas of compromise with Bush and the Republicans to get things done."[35]

Even as Democrats assume the mantle of the "loyal opposition," they cannot remain on one side of the values divide by appealing to single, unmarried, mostly urban, and nonwhite voters. Al Gore sensed this and published a 2002 book with his wife, Tipper, on the state of the American family.[36] While preaching values, Democrats must do a better job of making sure that traditional families—that is, those with working dads and stay-at-home moms—are welcomed into the party and that the values choices they have made are respected.

As Democrats seek to rehabilitate their image, party leaders must also have a compelling values story to tell. However, the word "values" cannot be repeated in mantra-like fashion, with the idea that mere repetition fixes the problem. Democrats must pay attention to both the language of values and its meaning. Bob Edgar, the general secretary of the National Council of Churches and a former Democratic congressman, understands that this can be accomplished within the context of a traditional progressive message:

The good news about the bad news was that the spin doctors, whether they got it right or wrong, have said that values are so important to our political system. They've given us an opportunity for us to say, "We're people of faith, too, and we're going to talk about what the Bible says about poverty." When nine million children are living in poverty, that's a moral value.[37]

Jim Wallis, author of the best-selling book *God's Politics: Why the Right Gets It Wrong and the Left Doesn't Get It*, agrees: "The perception of evangelicals is that all they care about is abortion and gay marriage, but it isn't true."[38] Elizabeth Theoharis, a community activist and doctoral student at Union Theological Seminary in New York City, summarizes the challenge: "How do we move from the idea of poor people being sinners to poverty being a sin?"[39]

The transition called for by Theoharis may be an especially difficult one for Democrats to make, as Democrats have been conditioned to think in terms of policies and programs rather than values—a tendency that dates back to the New Deal. At the onset of his 1932 presidential campaign, Franklin D. Roosevelt declared that, if elected, he would embark on a pattern of "bold and persistent experimentation" to cure the Great Depression. Roosevelt's plan was simple: "It is common sense to take a method and try it. If it fails, admit it frankly and try another. But above all, try something."[40] Roosevelt's bold experiments caused Democrats to think programmatically—that is, to offer voters a litany of government-run solutions to present-day problems. Laundry lists are beloved by prime ministers. But presidents are a different story, as Americans respond to values stories told to them by their presidents and party leaders. Republicans understand this and they have no problem speaking *thematically* rather than programmatically.

In sum, it is not enough for Democrats to say, "The issues are with us." While that is often the case, it is not enough to win. A February 2005 Zogby International poll makes the point. The survey found Democrats had a 14-point lead over the Republicans on handling healthcare, a 23-point advantage on protecting the environment, a 5-point advantage on jobs and the economy, and a 3-point edge on managing foreign policy. The same poll also found the public giving George W. Bush very negative marks on many of these same issues: 61 percent disapproved of

his handling of the Iraq War; 62 percent disliked the way he was dealing with jobs and the economy; 63 percent objected to his Social Security and Medicare plans; 60 percent disapproved of his handling of
education; 61 percent disliked his environmental policies; 56 percent
objected to his foreign policy; and 54 percent disliked his tax programs. Yet, respondents preferred Bush over Kerry by a margin of 46
percent to 42 percent, with 7 percent favoring a third-party candidate.[41] Clearly, people are not thinking programmatically when they
continue to prefer Bush over Kerry. Four months after the 2004 election, there was very little "buyer's remorse" from the voters over the
election results, even though the public disliked much of Bush's job
performance.

The February 2005 Zogby International poll and others like it
strongly suggest that the internal Democratic Party debate about
whether to move to the left or grab the center does not address the
party's main dilemma. On issue after issue, voters are comfortable with
progressive positions but do not know what the Democratic Party stands
for—or whether it stands for anything at all—because of the party's failure to present voters with a values narrative. The problem can be recti-
fied if Democrats begin articulating progressive values and stop worry-
ing about ideological positioning. Until Democrats learn to think and
speak *thematically*, watch for more disillusioning survey results and dis-
appointing Election Nights.

By addressing values, Democrats can reconnect with voters. One of
the ironies of American politics during the past decade is that economic
well-being is no longer connected to a party's values standing. Voters
suffered economically during Bush's first term, but many were unwilling
to give the Democrats a hearing because they believed Democratic candidates did not share their values. That old sign in the 1992 Clinton
headquarters that read "It's the economy, stupid!" no longer applies. But
Democrats have yet to comprehend this. When they figure out how to
talk to voters about progressive values, they will begin to address the values divide and win national elections. Until then, Democrats are poised
to lose elections even when the issues are with them. As Tom Robbins
wrote in his novel *Even Cowgirls Get the Blues*, "Until humans can solve
their philosophical problems, they're condemned to solve their political
problems over and over again. It's a cruel, repetitious bore."[42]

NOTES

1. Michael Waldman, *Potus Speaks: Finding the Words that Defined the Clinton Presidency* (New York: Simon and Schuster, 2000), 181.
2. John Kenneth White, *The New Politics of Old Values* (Hanover, N.H.: University Press of New England, 1990), passim.
3. John Kenneth White, interview with Richard B. Wirthlin, Washington, D.C., November 22, 1988.
4. Quoted in "Flawed Vision," *Washington Post*, August 21, 1988. According to the article, Reagan never received such a letter. Instead, the words had been penned nineteen years earlier by Mark Hawley in an essay printed in *Scouting Magazine* in 1969.
5. Accounts of this session are taken from Donald Morrison, ed., *The Winning of the White House, 1988* (New York: Time, 1988), 219; and "How Bush Won: The Inside Story of Campaign '88," *Newsweek*, November 21, 1988, 100.
6. Garry Wills, "Introduction," in Morrison, *Winning of the White House*, 5.
7. Bill Clinton, Acceptance Speech to the Democratic National Convention, July 16, 1992.
8. Bill Clinton, Farewell Address, January 18, 2001.
9. ABC News/*Washington Post* poll, August 26–30, 1992.
10. CBS News poll, August 18–19, 1992.
11. CBS News/*New York Times* poll, September 9–13, 1992.
12. Elizabeth Drew, *Showdown: The Struggle between the Gingrich Congress and the Clinton White House* (New York: Simon and Schuster, 1996), 202.
13. Bill Clinton, State of the Union Address, January 24, 1995.
14. Mark Penn and Doug Schoen, "Clinton: It Is Simply a Matter of Packaging," October 1995 memorandum, reprinted in Evan Thomas et al., *Back from the Dead: How Clinton Survived the Republican Revolution* (New York: Atlantic Monthly Press, 1997), 235–36.
15. Gallup poll, September 15–17, 1996.
16. The Tarrance Group and Mellman, Lazarus and Lake poll, January 27–29, 1996.
17. Peter D. Hart Research Associates poll, March 16–20, 1999.
18. Anna Greenberg and Stanley B. Greenberg, "Adding Values," *American Prospect*, August 28, 2000, 28.
19. CBS News/*New York Times* poll, February 12–14, 2000.
20. The "values voters" data are cited in David S. Broder and Richard Morin, "Worries about Nation's Morals Test a Reluctance to Judge," *Washington Post*, September 11, 1998.
21. Princeton Survey Research Associates poll, August 10–12, 2000.

22. ABC News/*Washington Post* poll, September 4–6, 2000, and CNN/*USA Today*/Gallup poll, August 11–12, 2000.

23. ABC News/*Washington Post* poll, September 4–6, 2000.

24. CBS News/*New York Times* poll, July 20–23, 2000; Greenberg Quinlan Research poll, September 4–9, 2000; and Princeton Survey Research Associates poll, August 24–September 10, 2000.

25. NBC News/*Wall Street Journal* poll, August 10–11, 2000.

26. Greenberg Quinlan Research poll, September 4–9, 2000.

27. John F. Kerry, Acceptance Speech to the Democratic National Convention, July 29, 2004.

28. See http://www.cbsnews.com/elements/2004/07/23/in_depth_politics/whoswho631596_0_15_person.shtml.

29. Zogby International Iowa tracking polls, January 8–10, 2004, and January 16–18, 2004.

30. NBC News/*Wall Street Journal* poll, December 9–13, 2004.

31. National Election Pool exit poll, November 2, 2004.

32. "Bush Ad Twists Kerry's Words on Iraq," FactCheck.org, September 28, 2004, http://factcheck.org/article269.html.

33. Stanley B. Greenberg and James Carville, "Toward a Democratic Purpose: A Survey and Resource for Democrats Taking Stock," Democracy Corps, February 1, 2005, 4, available at http://www.democracycorps.com/reports/analyses/Toward_a_Democratic_Purpose.pdf.

34. Democracy Corps poll, January 16–20, 2005. On this characteristic, 27 percent chose the Democrats; 55 percent picked the Republicans.

35. Gallup poll, survey of 223 members of the Democratic National Committee, January 27–February 8, 2005.

36. Al and Tipper Gore, *Joined at the Heart: The Transformation of the American Family* (New York: Henry Holt, 2002).

37. John Leland, "One More 'Moral Value': Fighting Poverty," *New York Times*, January 30, 2005.

38. Leland, "One More 'Moral Value.'" See also Jim Wallis, *God's Politics: Why the Right Gets It Wrong and the Left Doesn't Get It* (San Francisco: HarperSanFrancisco, 2005).

39. Leland, "One More 'Moral Value.'"

40. Franklin D. Roosevelt, Oglethorpe University Commencement Address, May 22, 1932.

41. Zogby International poll, February 25–27, 2005.

42. Tom Robbins, *Even Cowgirls Get the Blues* (Boston: Houghton Mifflin, 1976), quoted in Daniel Yankelovich, *New Rules: Searching for Self-Fulfillment in a World Turned Upside Down* (New York: Random House, 1981), preface.

5

SEEKING THE COMMON GOOD

Jim Wallis

Prophecy is not future telling, but articulating moral truth. The prophets diagnose the present and point the way to a just solution. The "prophetic tradition," in all of the world's great religions, is just what we need to open up our contemporary political options, which are, honestly, grossly failing to solve our most pressing social problems. The competing ideological options, from which we are forced to choose, are perhaps at their lowest ebb in compelling the involvement of ordinary citizens in public life. It is not that people just don't care, but that they feel unrepresented and unable to vote for anything that expresses their best values. That is a serious political crisis, and we need better options.

What would it mean to evaluate the leading current political options by the values of the prophets? What would happen if we asserted that values are the most important subject for the future of politics? What if we proposed a "prophetic politics?"

After the 2002 midterm elections, I attended a private dinner for Harvard Fellows in Cambridge. Our speaker was a Republican political strategist who had just won all the major senatorial and gubernatorial election campaigns in which he was involved. Needless to say, he was full of his success and eager to tell us about it. This very smart political operative said that Republicans won middle-class and even working-class people on the "social" issues, those moral and cultural issues that

Democrats don't seem to understand or appreciate. He even suggested that passion on the social issues can cause people to vote against their economic self-interest. Since the rich are already with us, he said, we win elections.

I raised my hand and asked the following question: "What would you do if you faced a candidate who took a traditional moral stance on the social and cultural issues? They would not be mean-spirited and, for example, blame gay people for the breakdown of the family, nor would they criminalize the choices of desperate women backed into difficult and dangerous corners. But the candidate would decidedly be pro-family, pro-life (meaning really want to lower the abortion rate), strong on personal responsibility and moral values, and outspoken against the moral pollution throughout popular culture that makes raising children in America a countercultural activity. And what if that candidate was also an economic populist, pro-poor in social policy, tough on corporate corruption and power, clear in supporting middle- and working-class families in health care and education, an environmentalist, and committed to a foreign policy that emphasized international law and multilateral cooperation over preemptive and unilateral war? What would you do?" I asked. He paused for a long time and then said, "We would panic!"

Virtually every time I'm out speaking on "prophetic politics" during any election year campaign, somebody asks the following question: "How can I vote for what I've just heard?" Some very interesting polling in the last few years shows how increasingly important voters' perceptions of "values" are to their electoral behavior. And most voters feel they can't really vote for their values, at least not all their values. In the polling, the values question now goes beyond traditional family and sexual matters and now also includes matters such as "caring for the poor." The problem is that politics is still run by ideological polarities that leave many people feeling left out.

There are now three major political options in our public life. The first political option in America today is conservative on everything—from cultural, moral, and family concerns to economic, environmental, and foreign policy issues. Differences emerge between aggressive nationalists and cautious isolationists, corporate apologists and principled fiscal conservatives, but this is the political option clearly on the ascendancy in America, with most of the dominant ideas in the public square coming from the political Right.

SEEKING THE COMMON GOOD

The second political option in contemporary America is liberal on everything—both family/sexual/cultural questions and economic, environmental, and foreign policy matters. There are certainly differences among the liberals (from pragmatic centrists to green leftists), but the intellectual and ideological roots come from the Left side of the cultural and political spectrum—and today most from the liberal/Left find themselves on the defensive.

The third option in American politics is libertarian, meaning liberal on cultural/moral issues and conservative on fiscal/economic and foreign policy. The "just leave me alone and don't spend my money option" is growing quickly in American life.

I believe there is a "fourth option" for American politics. It is traditional or conservative on issues of family values, sexual integrity and personal responsibility, while being very progressive, populist, or even radical on issues like poverty and racial justice. It affirms good stewardship of the earth and its resources, supports gender equality, and is more internationally minded than nationalist—looking first to peacemaking and conflict resolution when it comes to foreign policy questions. The people it appeals to (many religious, but others not) are very strong on issues like marriage, raising kids, and individual ethics, but without being right-wing, reactionary, or mean-spirited or scapegoating against any group of people, such as homosexuals. They can be pro-life, pro-family, and pro-feminist, all at the same time. They think issues of "moral character" are very important, both in a politician's personal life and in his or her policy choices. Yet they are decidedly pro-poor, for racial reconciliation, critical of purely military solutions, and defenders of the environment.

At the heart of the fourth option is the integral link between personal ethics and social justice. And it appeals to people who refuse to make the choice between the two.

Who are these people? Many are religious: Catholics, black and Hispanic Christians, evangelicals who don't identify with the religious Right, and members of all our denominational churches who want to put their faith into practice. They are Jews and Muslims who are guided by an active faith and not just a personal background. They are people who do not consider themselves religious, but rather spiritual. And they are people—religious, spiritual, or not—who consider themselves shaped by a strong sense of moral values and who long for a political commitment that reflects them.

As I travel the country, I find many people who share this perspective. Still, it is not yet a political option. It should be. As one who has called for a new moral politics that transcends the old categories of both the secular Left and the religious Right, I believe it is time to assert a clear fourth political option. In a recent conversation I had with E. J. Dionne of the *Washington Post*, the columnist said there was a huge constituency of "non-right-wing Christians" and other morally concerned people in the country who need to get organized. Like E. J., they are moderate to conservative on personal moral questions and very progressive on social justice.

Recent polling shows that the more religious voters are, the more likely they are to vote for the conservatives. Given how negatively much of the political Left seems to regard religion and spirituality, this is not surprising. But what if a new political option regarded personal ethics to be as important as social justice and saw faith as a positive force in society—for progressive social change? I think the fourth option could be a real winning vision, and I believe many are very hungry for it. While the political elites and many special-interest groups resist the personal ethics/social justice combination (perhaps because it threatens many special interests), many ordinary people would welcome it.

What we need is nothing less than prophetic politics. We must find a new moral and political language that transcends old divisions and seeks the common good. Prophetic politics finds its center in fundamental moral issues like children, diversity, family, community, citizenship, and ethics (others could be added, like nonviolence, tolerance, and fairness) and tries to construct national directions that many people across the political spectrum could agree to. It would speak directly to the proverb quoted earlier, "Without a vision, the people perish," and would offer genuine political vision that arises out of biblical passages from prophetic texts. Our own ancient prophetic religious traditions could offer a way forward beyond our polarized and paralyzed national politics and could be the foundation for a fourth political option to provide the new ideas politics always needs.

The political class is at war, while the media focus more on the process of politics than its content. And while there are certainly very committed partisans on both sides, they seem to be fighting more for their careers than their principles. In the meantime, most Americans are not terribly passionate about their political choices. During election season, many voters are undecided until the very end, speak in "lesser of evils" language about their decisions, and wonder if this is really the best America has to offer.

Most simply put, the two traditional options in America (Democrat and Republican, liberal and conservative) have failed to capture the imagination, commitment, and trust of a clear majority of people in this country. Neither has found ways to solve our deepest and most entrenched social problems. Record prosperity hasn't cured child poverty. Family breakdown is occurring across all class and racial lines. Public education remains a disaster for millions of families. Millions more still don't have health insurance or can't find affordable housing. The environment suffers from unresolved debates, while our popular culture becomes more and more polluted by violent and sex-saturated "entertainment." In local communities, people are more and more isolated, busy, and disconnected. Our foreign policy has become an aggressive assertion of military superiority in a defensive and reactive mode, seeking to protect us against growing and invisible threats instead of addressing the root causes of those threats. The political Right and Left continue at war with each other, but the truth is that these false ideological choices themselves have run their course and become dysfunctional.

Prophetic politics would not be an endless argument between personal and social responsibility, but a weaving of the two together in search of the common good. The current options are deadlocked. Prophetic politics wouldn't assign all the answers to the government, the market, or the churches and charities, but rather would patiently and creatively forge new civic partnerships in which everyone does their share and everybody does what they do best. Prophetic politics wouldn't debate whether our strategies should be cultural, political, or economic but would show how they must be all three, led by a moral compass.

Perhaps most importantly, prophetic politics won't be led just by elected officials, lawyers, and their financial backers. Look for community organizers, social entrepreneurs, nonprofit organizations, faith-based communities, and parents to help show the way forward now. Pay particular attention to a whole generation of young people forged in community service. They may be cynical about politics, but they are vitally concerned with public life. The politics we need now will arise more from building social and spiritual movements than from merely lobbying at party conventions. And ultimately, it will influence the party conventions, as successful movements always do.

The prophetic role churches are now undertaking is illustrative of the larger public vocation that may now be required. That role has become more clear in the wake of the election. Without a clear and compelling vision, Democrats had nothing to offer the American people as an alternative to the Bush administration.

With the Republicans offering war overseas and corporate dominance at home, and the Democrats failing to offer any real alternatives, who will raise a prophetic voice for social and economic justice and for peace? Never has there been a clearer role for the churches and religious community. We can push both parties toward moral consistency and their best-stated values and away from the unprincipled pragmatism and negative campaigning that both sides too often engaged in during the recent election.

The courage many church leaders showed in opposing the war with Iraq is an early sign of that prophetic role. So is the growing unity across the spectrum of the churches on the issue of poverty. The truth is that there are more churches committed to justice and peace than belong to the religious Right. It's time the voice of those congregations be heard and their activism be mobilized to become the conscience of American politics in a time of crisis.

We have seen many moments in recent history when the churches emerged as the leading voice of political conscience. Certainly there were key times in the South African struggle against apartheid when the churches there became the critical public voice both for political challenge and for change. Leaders such as Desmond Tutu, Alan Boesak, and Frank Chikane served as both church and public figures at the same time. Who can forget the role of Archbishop Oscar Romero in El Salvador during the 1980s, church leaders in the Philippines during the revolution that ousted dictator Ferdinand Marcos, or the critical opposition to communist rule in Poland? In many other oppressive circumstances, churches and church leaders have risen to the call to prophetic public leadership.

Even in democracies, churches have responded to that same prophetic vocation. In New Zealand during the 1990s, when conservative forces ripped that society's long-standing social safety net to pieces, it was the churches in partnership with the indigenous Maori people who led marches, ignited public protest, and emboldened a wobbly Labour party to recapture the government and restore key programs in health care, housing, and social services. And, of course, it was in the United States that black churches, under the leadership of Baptist ministers such as Reverend Martin Luther King Jr., provided the moral foundation and social infrastructure for a powerful civil rights movement that reminded the nation of its expressed ideals and changed us forever.

In a bitterly divided nation, we face historic challenges. But the political "tie" that the nation is caught in might be a moment of opportunity. It shows that the old options and debates have created a deadlock. This very crisis could open the way for some new and creative thinking and organizing. And that could be very good news indeed. Our political leaders must learn the wisdom that the way to reach common ground is to move to higher ground. And we citizens should start by showing the way.

VOTING ALL YOUR VALUES

With religious fundamentalists on one side and secular fundamentalists on the other, how should religious people express their vision of faith and politics? How do we do more than conform to existing options and instead help create better alternatives for solving the pressing problems of our society? And, most particularly, how are we to vote?

First, we should ask what the religious profession of candidates actually means for their policy making. If religious affirmation is not tied to real political values and directions, what good is the expression of such public piety? And how could genuine discussion of moral, spiritual, or religious values in public life contribute to the formation of needed new political options?

When George Bush said in the 2000 presidential campaign that Jesus was "his favorite philosopher," it was fair to ask what that meant for his political philosophy. Would the poor get prioritized on his policy agenda as they did with Jesus? And the same with Al Gore's claim that he often asked himself "What would Jesus do?" Which candidate's political commitments were more likely to focus on the bottom 20 percent of American families, including thirteen million children who are living in poverty and shut out of our national well-being? Bush should have been asked if child poverty would get more attention in his administration than oil and gas interests; Gore should have been asked how he would implement his new populist rhetoric when it inevitably collided with the interests of the corporations that now finance both political parties. It's an appropriate moral concern to ask candidates about their plans to extend health care and education to those without them. And protecting the environment is as much a religious issue as caring for the poor. What if religious voters asked which candidates see human rights and workers' protections to be as important as global trade?

How does the religious principle of the sacredness of human life challenge all the candidates, for example, on abortion, capital punishment, military spending, missile defense, or gun control? Religious people may disagree on the answers to those questions (for example, Joe Lieberman supports both capital punishment and legal abortion while the Catholic bishops do not), but shouldn't the highest rates of both abortion and death-row executions in the Western world be a concern to all those who profess moral values? Couldn't both pro-life and pro-choice political leaders agree to common ground actions that would actually reduce the abortion rate, rather than continue to use abortion mostly as a political symbol? Instead of imposing rigid pro-choice and pro-life political litmus tests, why not work together on teen pregnancy, adoption reform, and real alternatives for women backed into dangerous and lonely corners? Do we really want to dramatically reduce abortion and make it "rare," as Bill Clinton once suggested, or have both sides just continue to treat this deeply important issue as a political football? And here is another tough values question for both parties: How does allegiance to the Christian Prince of Peace or the God of the Hebrew prophets square with a national security policy that still relies on threatening the use of nuclear weapons—something all of our religious traditions abhor? What does the same "sacredness of human life" principle mean for foreign and military policy?

Chicago's late Catholic cardinal Joseph Bernardin often spoke of a "seamless garment" of life, which applied to any issue where human lives are at stake, from abortion and euthanasia, to capital punishment and nuclear weapons, to poverty and racism. Applying that consistent life ethic to politics would upset the ideological apple carts of both Republicans and Democrats, which would be a very good role for the religious community.

Speaking of moral concerns, whose policies will better strengthen family life and values (something both liberal and conservative households with children could support), combat the spread of violence both in the popular culture and on our streets, and advance racial justice and reconciliation? Moral character and leadership are important. The attempted separation of personal and public behavior by occupants of the White House doesn't square well with biblical religion or make most of us very happy about the message our kids are getting.

How does one distinguish between symbolic choices and responsible ones? Is voting for candidates who are far from perfect—"the lesser of evils"—a moral compromise or an ethical decision to seek incremental change? The answers to these questions are far from easy. But sorting out the meaning of faith in the world seldom is. One thing is clear: True faith cannot be kept inside the narrow boundaries of the "sacred," as some would suggest, but is intended to be "salt and light" in the midst of what is often called the secular world. Indeed, to change the world is a vocation of faith. Elections are not the most important part of that, but they are indeed one significant piece of faithful citizenship in a political democracy. So think, pray—and then vote.

It is important to remember that the particular religiosity of a candidate, or even how devout they might be, is less important than how their religious and/or moral commitments and values shape their political vision and their policy commitments. If one's religious and ethical convictions don't shape a candidate's (or a citizen's) public life—what kind of commitments are they? Yet in a democratic and pluralistic society, we don't want to evaluate candidates by which denomination or faith tradition they belong to (and only vote for the candidate in our group) or how often they attended church or synagogue (like a tally of votes missed by a member of Congress), but rather to understand the moral compass they bring to their public life and how their convictions shape their political priorities.

There were some positive signs among the Democrats in the 2004 campaign. While Howard Dean's initial forays into religion were clumsy at best (surely someone on his staff must have known that his "favorite

New Testament book" of Job was, in fact, in the Old Testament), his concern about losing our "sense of community" in America was a deeply moral and religious one. Perhaps knowing what is contained in the books of the Bible is ultimately more important than knowing where they all are! Dick Gephardt talked about health care as a "moral issue," and John Edwards, who became the Democratic candidate for vice president, sounded like a preacher when he spoke of two Americas and declared that poverty is not only an economic concern, but is "about right and wrong," and that "poverty reduction is a moral responsibility." Joe Lieberman seemed to be regaining his religious voice when he spoke about the poor, and John Kerry, who became candidate for president, was talking about a "broken value system" and not just his war record. Wesley Clark seemed to be comfortable relating his faith journey to social justice, Dennis Kucinich spoke of his moral values all along the campaign trail, and of course, Reverend Al Sharpton spoke like the Pentecostal preacher he is. As we've noted earlier, Kerry and Edwards spoke more strongly about their faith as the campaign wore on. George Bush continued to speak of his personal faith as a motivator and was pushed to be more explicit about how his personal faith applied to social issues like HIV/AIDS.

Perhaps the most mistaken media perception of our time is that religious influence in politics only equates to the politics of the religious Right. The biggest story that the mainstream media has yet to discover is how much that reality is changing. My prediction is that moderate and progressive religious voices will ultimately shape politics in the coming decades far more significantly than the religious Right will.

First, it is a mistake to regard all the conservative Christians who are sympathetic to the religious Right as people who want to impose their religious values on fellow citizens. To be conservative is not necessarily to be fundamentalist. In my experience, most are motivated more by defensive feelings than offensive intentions. Many people of faith (of all different political stripes) are concerned about the coarsening of American life, the unraveling of traditional values, and threats to religious precepts like the sacredness of human life. What our children are being subjected to on television, in school yards, and now over the Internet has been a greater motivating force for political involvement than keeping the Ten Commandments in state courthouses or any number of other issues on the agenda of the political right wing.

It is true that some of the religious Right's leaders are indeed theocrats—those who would impose their versions of morality on the nation if they ever had the chance. Their mistake was the attempt to take political power in and through the Republican Party to impose a "moral" agenda from the top down. But even more disconcerting has been what is missing from the agenda of the religious Right—such as concern for the poor and racial justice—and the appeals of the movement's leaders to affluent self-interest over biblical imperatives. How did tax cuts for the rich become a religious imperative? Those blatant hypocrisies of the religious Right are becoming more and more evident, especially to a new generation of evangelical Christians.

History does teach us that the most effective social movements are also spiritual ones, which change people's thinking and attitudes by appealing to moral and religious values. Those movements change the cultural and political climate, which then makes policy changes more possible, palatable, and, yes, democratic. The best example of doing it right, as we have said, is the American civil rights movement, which was led by ministers who appealed directly to biblical faith. I believe that will be the more likely pattern for future movements that combine faith and politics, replacing the more politically conformist model of the religious Right.

It is another mistake to be always fighting against the religious Right, as many frightened liberals continue to do. The electoral strength of the Moral Majority or the Christian Coalition was always exaggerated by both themselves and the media, but now their ability to "deliver" decisive blocs of votes is greatly diminished. The Republican Party is now careful at party conventions to hide its religious fundamentalists, as mainstream voters have soured on both their message and style.

There was indeed a period in the 1980s and 1990s when the perception abounded that "Christian" involvement in politics meant Christian Right. But that hasn't been true for some time now. The U.S. Catholic Conference of Bishops has provided real social policy leadership in the last decade and has become a clear alternative to the dominance of groups like the Moral Majority and the Christian Coalition. The Catholic bishops are opposed to abortion, but also to capital punishment, increased military spending, and notions of welfare reform that neglect poor working families.

Influential organizations like World Vision and World Relief are play-ing leadership roles in sensitizing and mobilizing evangelicals for disas-ter relief, comprehensive economic development, and global campaigns to combat HIV/AIDS. Influential groups like Evangelicals for Social Ac-tion led by Ron Sider, the Christian Community Development Associa-tion led by John Perkins, and the Evangelical Association for the Pro-motion of Education led by Tony and Bart Campolo, have defined poverty reduction as a compelling moral, biblical, and decidedly evan-gelical issue. Several conservative evangelical denominations, like the Evangelical Covenant Church, have now made the critical links be-tween evangelism, compassion, and social justice. Evangelical Christian colleges have shown a deepening social conscience in their curriculums over issues of poverty and race, often putting them at odds with the Evangelical right wing.

New leadership in the mainline Protestant churches also promises greater ecumenical collaboration on social issues with both evangelicals and Catholics. Many of those denominations have played critical lead-ership roles in faith-inspired movements like Jubilee 2000, a broad coalition for debt cancellation for the world's poorest countries, which has demonstrated a real impact on international governmental policy and has shown the power and potential for crossing old dividing lines in the religious community.

Overtly Christian organizations like Bread for the World (a nation-wide Christian citizens' movement seeking justice for the world's hun-gry people by lobbying our nation's decision makers) and Habitat for Humanity (a nonprofit, ecumenical Christian housing ministry) have demonstrated a strong advocacy for faith-based justice in the public square and have established a clear place for moderate and progressive religious perspectives. Call to Renewal has been successful in pulling the churches together on the issue of poverty across the wide spectrum of the church's life, thus offering another alternative to the Religious Right's silence on that issue. More and more Christians are openly ad-vocating the kind of biblically based social justice agenda that has long characterized the readers of magazines like *Sojourners* and *The Other Side*. Thus the religious Right is now only one of many voices on issues of political ethics, as it should be.

The public conversation about religious and moral values now has the potential to be a serious and thoughtful discussion in America. The good news for religion and public life in America is that the word *religious* will no longer always be followed by the word *Right.*

To move away from the bifurcating politics of liberal and conservative, left and right, would be an enormously positive change and would open up a new "politics of solutions." Right now, Washington responds to a problem or crisis in two ways. First, politicians try to make us afraid of the problem, and second, they look for somebody to blame for it. Then they watch to see whose political spin succeeded, either in the next poll or the next election. But they seldom get around to actually solving the problem. The media make everything worse by assuming that every political issue has only two sides, instead of multiple angles for viewing and solving the problem. Addicted to conflict as their media methodology, they want always to pitch a fight between polarized views instead of convening a public discussion to find serious answers. The answer is to put values at the center of political discourse and, in every public debate, to ask what kind of country and people we really want to be. We would find new agreements across old political boundaries and new common ground among people who agree on values and are ready to challenge the special interests on all sides who are obstructing the solutions most Americans would support. Ideologies have failed us; values can unite us, especially around our most common democratic visions.

6

CRAFTING POLICY AND MESSAGE

John Podesta and John Halpin

An effective message is short, clear, memorable, and resonant with voters. Message does not drive policy, it explains it; it is an accurate summary of and explanation for policy. Policy, in turn, is the product of contemporary challenges and firm, fundamental values.

With the emergence of modern polling techniques and precision targeting, progressives face the growing temptation to craft a message first, and then back-engineer in search of a compatible policy. This is a failed strategy: messages expressed outside of real values, without being rooted firmly in realistic policies, are both ineffective and meaningless. Our values and our history should provide the basis for effective policies that advance the progressive agenda, and for a message that makes progressive policy accessible and compelling to the voting public.

This chapter looks at those values and roots, and at the history of successful progressive policies, to help frame an overall progressive message and to begin connecting our core principles to the real problems Americans now face. We aim to suggest themes and policy ideas—grounded in time-honored progressive principles—for an emerging progressive agenda. We do not attempt to propagate a universal message for all progressive activists and leaders. Although we sympathize with the desire to create a progressive "bumper sticker" to battle the Right, our experience has taught us that anyone endeavoring to uncover the Rosetta Stone of progressive messaging is on a fool's errand.

Progressives throughout history have always differed on the key priorities, principles, and political strategies necessary for social change. Similarly, the conservative movement's political success is as much a result of the competition of deeply held convictions and policy prescriptions as it is a function of ideological tenets and goals repeated ad nauseam. If we want to move forward, progressives should focus less on message litmus tests and more on creating a robust climate for intellectual exchange, the development of new ideas, and genuine collaboration.

In this spirit, we suggest the following themes as a starting point for a more detailed look at progressive policy and message today:

- *Progressives believe that America is prosperous and strong when we provide opportunity to the middle class and have a system that rewards work and is open to all regardless of one's station in life. Our diversity is our strength, and all Americans should have the opportunity to realize their aspirations and ambitions through a meaningful and dignified life.*

- *Progressives believe that terrorism and weapons of mass destruction pose a real and present danger to our nation and that an aggressive national security strategy is required to defeat those dangers. We believe in a military that is second to none and have a willingness to use force to defend our national interest while also engaging the world through alliances with our friends abroad. We are serious about sharing and spreading American values and rebuilding America's economic strength as essential to safeguarding our nation.*

- *Progressives believe the privileges of American life for all must be accompanied by responsibilities from all and a genuine commitment to serve the larger community: citizens owe something to their families and localities; public officials to the national interest; and corporate leaders to shareholders, employees, consumers, and communities. Progressives recognize the responsibility to use the commonwealth for the common good and believe Americans have a duty to manage wisely the national and natural assets we hold in trust for future generations.*

PAST AS PROLOGUE

As we study the challenges of the twenty-first century, our history as progressives points us in the direction of solutions. The progressive impulse arose in response to disturbing trends in American life associated with rapid industrialization and the emergence of a powerful and uncontrolled capitalist economy during the latter nineteenth and early twentieth centuries. Progressive reformers sought to improve conditions for Americans by harnessing the power of the national government to assist the needy and vulnerable, to regulate and balance a rapidly developing capitalist economy, and to challenge totalitarian forces across the globe that threatened to undermine democracy and freedom.

The progressive response to insecurity and exploitation was a politics rooted in the core virtues of fairness, global leadership, and community:

- *Fairness.* Progressives worked to create the legal, political, and economic conditions that would allow individuals to use their abilities and aspirations to make the most of their lives. Fairness required government action to protect basic rights and liberties for every American, to level the economic playing field, and to provide basic services and opportunities. But citizens had obligations as well: to treat people with respect, to understand different backgrounds and views, and to avoid self-interested actions and beliefs that unfairly harm others. Fairness did not guarantee that everybody would be the same, think the same, or get the same material benefits in life. It simply attempted to guarantee a fair shot at success.
- *Global leadership.* Progressivism focused on protecting American interests and extending American values on a global scale, with economic power, military might, and moral strength. Progressives led the fight to make the world safe for democracy by opposing fascism and communism on every continent. Progressives relied on military power, but had an integrated national security strategy that included moral leadership, alliance building, burden sharing, and strong public diplomacy.
- *Community.* Progressives believed that community strength is more important than narrow economic self-interest. The focus on community provided progressives with a sense of national purpose

and placed citizenship at the heart of successful democratic governance. It asked business and corporate interests to recognize the
impact of their decisions on workers, localities, and the environment. The progressive focus on community also recognized the
importance of bringing politics back to the people and on creating
an active and engaged citizenry imbued with a sense of duty and
sacrifice to society and country. Most importantly, progressives believed that citizens and leaders alike must give something back by
staying involved in the affairs of their community, voting, voicing
opinions, volunteering, and placing the country's needs above narrow self-interest.

With these values as a platform for a political agenda, progressives set
the stage for America's emergence as a global power.

As the challenges in early twentieth-century American life grew
larger, progressives—primarily through the philosophical analysis of
Herbert Croly and the political leadership of Teddy Roosevelt—har-
nessed expanded federal influence as a means for bettering society and
balancing corporate dominance.[1] The progressive ideal of using "Hamil-
tonian means to achieve Jeffersonian ends" was carried out to create a
strong national government that promoted democratic values and increased economic opportunities for all citizens.

The New Deal, the Fair Deal, and other domestic progressive initiatives allowed citizens, through their national government, to correct severe economic and racial injustices that individuals and the private
economy alone could not address. Just a short list of major progressive
accomplishments includes: dramatically expanding public education;
developing fair and safe working conditions; supporting unionization
and the minimum wage; building public transportation and highways;
establishing national parks and protected lands; cleaning our air and water; expanding voting rights; weaving a social safety net anchored by Social Security, Medicare, and Medicaid; ensuring safer food and drugs;
funding world-class medical advancements and scientific achievements;
writing the GI Bill; embracing the civil rights movement; and launching
the space program.

On the international front, progressive presidents such as Wilson and
Truman supported strong military and diplomatic intervention to make

the world safer for Americans, to defend our values, to promote freedom and democracy, and to improve the conditions of people around the globe. Progressives' foreign policy accomplishments include fighting and winning two world wars and the Cold War, creating the Marshall Plan, building the postwar international trading system, pushing for international human rights treaties, and helping to liberate tens of millions of people worldwide from poverty and oppression.

But as John Judis points out in the *New Republic*, progressive reformers in the twenty-first century face different challenges than their predecessors: a global economy with new rules; shifting employment patterns; demands on public programs; a decline in the power of intermediary organizations such as labor unions; and the rejection of regulatory and tax policies by American business and multinational corporations.[2]

New realities limit the application of past policies to current situations. Twenty-first-century progressives face ongoing threats from extremists and terrorists across the globe that are far different than the totalitarian and communist threats we battled in the twentieth century. In key areas, the limits of government power have been tested, and perhaps exceeded. The private sector is recognized as the primary engine of economic growth. The importance of strong moral values, personal responsibility, and entrepreneurship in resolving social pathologies is widely understood.

At the same time, almost a century of progressive reform proves that, in some roles, government's effectiveness can no longer be seriously questioned. The progressive track record includes effective government action in increasing access to quality health care, improving public education, providing a safe and sound retirement for the elderly, and protecting the environment.

Today's leaders and citizens face a world of once unimaginable economic opportunities—and competition for jobs and profits from every corner of the earth. The American military is the most powerful in history—yet we are not sure how to deploy it against terrorist cells and small rogue states. Our economy is growing—but more and more middle-class families are losing access to jobs, health care, and affordable housing. In the information age, government secrecy is on the rise. Individuals are being asked to take full responsibility for their lives, while large institutions seem increasingly eager to avoid taking any responsibility at all.

The progressive challenge in the twenty-first century is to resolve these contradictions in ways that accord with our values and make America stronger, more affluent, and more secure.

DEFENDING A NEW PROGRESSIVISM

The values of fairness, global leadership, and community remain strong progressive ideals. But contemporary events demand that they evolve, as our world has evolved, to meet the challenges of the twenty-first century. We must apply traditional progressive values to the following questions:

1. *How do we as Americans continue to improve our living standards and ensure broad-based economic opportunities in a rapidly changing and frequently unstable global economy?*
2. *How do democratic nations across the globe coalesce to defeat terrorism and religious extremism?*
3. *How can we reform our political system to ensure honesty, openness, and democratic commitment worthy of the public's respect and admiration?*

With history as our guide and our values as the foundation of a progressive political vision, we have an opportunity to put forth a new and compelling message that meets the conditions of the twenty-first century and gives people hope for a better future by strengthening the middle class, asserting global leadership, and reforming our political system to better serve the American people.

Goal One: Strengthen the Middle Class

Progressives believe that America is prosperous and strong when we provide opportunity to the middle class and have a system that rewards work and is open to all regardless of one's station in life. Our diversity is our strength, and all Americans should have the opportunity to realize their aspirations and ambitions through a meaningful and dignified life.

Rather than valuing and rewarding work, conservative economic policies reward concentrations of wealth and privilege and stifle the progress of middle-class Americans by shifting the tax burden onto their backs, cutting wages for their jobs, and ending medical and retirement benefits for their old age.

A new progressive agenda will honor and support work by promoting quality education, home ownership, a fair tax system, and health care for all. We will make sure that public resources are available to promote private growth; from basic infrastructure to advanced technology, we will ensure that American individuals and businesses have the tools they need to compete in the world economy. We will ensure that our open and growing economy benefits all by recognizing our social responsibilities to those threatened by change.

The Conservative Legacy

Wrong Choices. Wrong Priorities. President Bush and Congress squandered historic budget surpluses that could have saved Social Security. They have spent billions on a war in Iraq that is plagued by mismanagement and lack of planning. They've racked up huge trade deficits and mortgaged our children's future to foreign banks and governments.

The revenue lost to the government from the 2001–2003 tax cuts is three times the amount that would have been needed to make the Social Security system solvent for the next seventy-five years.[3] Persistent deficits are a long-term drain on the economy, and with foreign governments holding massive amounts of American debt, we are concerned about instability in the international finance and trade arenas. Massive debt amounts to a birth tax on future generations and irresponsibly ignores long-term imbalances in the system.

Tax cuts for the wealthy matched with runaway spending have turned a $236 billion federal surplus into a $427 billion deficit.[4] This leads to higher interest rates that will make it harder for families to buy a home, get out of debt, and—for too many—fend off bankruptcies or foreclosures.

Cutting Investment in What Keeps America Strong. Conservative priorities have made the struggle of the middle class even more of a challenge: jobs are going overseas; quality health care is increasingly out of reach; educational opportunities are down; and the tax system is rigged to help not them but big corporations and the top 1 percent of wage earners instead. Communities, public safety, schools, health care, and retirement are being sacrificed.

Right-wing leaders have forced massive cuts and harsh caps on discretionary spending and entitlements. Cuts in education funding make it more difficult for middle-class students to afford college and find a well-paying job. The prescription drug bill, passed in 2004, helps the pharmaceutical industry at the expense of seniors, while healthcare costs continue to skyrocket. All of this is happening while median household incomes and wages are stagnating.

Major investment cuts in the president's 2006 budget include:[5]

- *Medicaid.* The budget sought to cut Medicaid by up to $60 billion over ten years, which would have shifted enormous costs to the states.
- *Education.* The budget called for reducing discretionary spending authority for the Department of Education by 1 percent and proposed eliminating federal funding for forty-eight education programs.
- *Environment.* The budget cut total funding for natural resources and the environment by 11 percent. It cut the EPA budget by 6 percent, cut clean water funding by $700 million, and included a backdoor provision for drilling in the Arctic National Wildlife Refuge.

We Now See Who and What Conservatives Really Value. Conservative tax policy is utterly bereft of vision and values. At a time when the president and congressional leaders are asking American soldiers and middle-class taxpayers to sacrifice for the country, they are telling corporations and the wealthy that they owe nothing and have no obligation to support the national interest. Right-wing leaders are giving them tax breaks for doing nothing.

Fiscal outrages in the president's 2006 budget include:[6]

- *Permanent extension of tax cuts.* Most of the president's tax cuts are set to expire in or before 2010. The policies that have yet to be extended overwhelmingly benefit those who are very wealthy, saving

$150,000 annually for those making more than $1 million a year while yielding middle-income taxpayers virtually nothing. These tax changes will cost the federal government hundreds of billions of dollars in lost revenue.

- *Wealth over work.* The president's proposals continue to give preferential treatment for income generated from capital gains at the expense of wage earners. Extending tax reductions for capital gains and dividends will cost $162 billion over ten years. Eliminating the estate tax will cost $256 billion over ten years. Almost all of the benefits from the estate tax repeal go to a sliver of the wealthiest Americans.

A Progressive Agenda

In sharp contrast to the conservative platform and record, progressive economic policy will bring Americans together, invest in the nation's future, and reward work.

Bring Americans Together. America is stronger when a secure and growing middle class is recognized as essential to the economic security of our nation, when economic policies are fair, and when budgetary decisions are driven by the values of fairness, compassion, and respect for others.

- *Achieve universal health care coverage by 2010.* The failure of our society and government to provide basic health care coverage to 45 million Americans is a moral and economic failure of the first order. Every year, uninsured individuals pay $33 billion out of pocket for health care, with the overall health system absorbing an additional $41 billion in "uncompensated" care costs—costs eventually passed on to others.[7] Health and longevity losses, including educational disruptions and developmental delays in children with untreated illnesses, total as much as $130 billion per year.[8]

Progressives can develop a comprehensive and financially sound program that both builds upon the existing health system and creates new ways to make universal health coverage attainable and affordable. Three principles should guide the process: practicality, fairness, and responsibility. Rather than re-create the health system—a tremendous challenge

for a sector that constitutes nearly 15 percent of our nation's output—
we should build on the existing employer-based system and find areas of
consensus among government officials and the private sector, which
shoulders a large share of the healthcare burden. Coverage must be affordable and accessible to all, irrespective of health, age, income, or
work status, but workers must participate in and help fund the program.
Most importantly, the plan must have viable financing options to be self-
sustaining.

Invest in America's Future. Working together, we must recommit
ourselves and our resources to building and investing in people, research, technology, training, and workplace environments that can keep
the American economy strong.

- *Ensure that every public school student in America is taught by
  highly qualified, well-trained, and adequately supported teachers.*
  Progressives should start by increasing the quality and quantity of
  information about America's teacher workforce and should encourage the use of such data for greater accountability and smarter decision making. This includes data to track teachers' strengths and
  weaknesses to help with professional development and better
  placement of teachers, as well as the enforcement of federal regulations requiring extensive reporting of teacher data. We must also
  create enriched career advancement structures that treat teaching
  as a clinical practice profession, much like medicine, and improve
  teacher recruitment and preparation in higher education. Congress
  should commit $1 billion in five states to invest in programs to pro-
  vide teachers with differentiated career development throughout
  their professional lives. We should provide targeted incentives and
  enforce existing laws to decrease inequities in access to qualified
  teachers and better match teacher skills with student needs. And
  we need to create instructional environments that maximize
  teacher effectiveness and reduce teacher turnover in high-poverty
  schools.
- *Redesign our schools to better prepare students for post–high
  school learning.* We must ensure that students are graduating from
  high school with the skills and knowledge necessary to earn post-
  secondary credentials. Progressives should consider pushing successful and innovative ideas for redesigning large high schools as

smaller learning communities; establishing charter schools that incorporate extended learning time and greater parental involvement; and creating early/middle college high schools that are located on college campuses and allow students to earn an associate's degree along with a high school diploma.

Reward Work. The heart of America has always been its middle class. America should reward individual initiative, ingenuity, and hard work and provide people with the economic and social opportunities to make the most of their talents and dreams.

- *Pursue tax policies that reward hard work and promote shared prosperity.* Progressives should push for reforms that would tax wage, salary, capital gains, and dividend income according to the same rate schedule. We should restructure and simplify the income tax by establishing a simple, progressive, three-rate structure and reduce the share of taxes collected from the regressive payroll tax. We should improve the Earned Income Tax Credit by expanding the number of families eligible to receive the federal child tax credit. Ultimately, progressive tax reform will increase the take-home pay of low- and middle-income families and generate the funds our country needs.
- *Simplify the tax code to help middle-class families.* Progressives should consider ways to simplify the tax structure by cutting the number of income tax brackets in half to three rates—15 percent, 25 percent, and 39.6 percent. Combined with the elimination of the employee portion of the payroll tax, most people will experience a tax cut, with those earning less than $200,000 averaging an increase of more than $1,000 in their take-home pay. Progressives should advocate eliminating the Alternative Minimum Tax (AMT), which, if left in place, will impact 36 million Americans by 2010.[9] The AMT was first established in 1969 to ensure that the wealthiest Americans do not avoid paying their fair share. While the AMT applied to only 9,000 people in 1970, its income limits are not indexed to inflation, so the number of individuals subjected to the AMT had grown to 1.3 million by 2000.[10] Since then, the number of people affected by the AMT has continued to increase, in part because the Bush tax policies lowered some taxes at the high end

but did not appropriately adjust the AMT. The AMT adds significant complexity to the tax-filing process, essentially forcing people to compute their taxes twice. Overhauling the income tax code would eliminate the need for an AMT, and thus address, in a fiscally responsible manner, a central tax challenge facing our country over the next decade.

- *Make corporations and the wealthy pay their fair share.* The complexity of the corporate income tax is hurting our competitiveness and encouraging companies to shift production overseas. By broadening the base of the corporate tax structure, we can enhance the overall efficiency of the system, keep rates at relatively low levels, and increase revenues. For example, the recently enacted $140 billion corporate tax overhaul includes a wide range of specialized credits that should be reexamined. Eliminating corporate tax loopholes and special giveaways to the wealthy would provide an estimated revenue gain of $30 billion annually.[11] In addition, by closing some of the most egregious loopholes, we would ensure that our tax code no longer offers affirmative incentives for wealthy individuals to shelter taxable income or for corporations to shift production outside the United States.

Goal Two: Assert Global Leadership

Progressives believe that terrorism and weapons of mass destruction pose a real and present danger to our nation and that an aggressive national security strategy is required to defeat those dangers. We believe in a military that is second to none and have a willingness to use force to defend our national interest while also engaging the world through alliances with our friends abroad. We are serious about sharing and spreading American values and rebuilding America's economic strength as essential to safeguarding our nation.

In opposing the myopic and counterproductive direction of current U.S. national security policies, progressives should not abandon their historical commitment to internationalism and the aggressive use of all tools in our arsenal—hard and soft—to advance American interests and security, improve world living conditions, and promote global peace and stability.

Conservatives, rather than protecting our citizens by spreading American ideals and offering American help to improve life in the developing world, rely instead on a go-it-alone defense strategy that stretches our military capacity, alienates our allies, hurts our brave enlisted men and women and their families, and neglects the needs of Americans at home.

U.S. operations in Iraq and Afghanistan have revealed deeply troubling cracks in the organization and structure of the million-strong U.S. Army. These problems have been exacerbated both by the current challenges of the international security environment and the way in which the Bush administration has used active-duty and reserve components since September 11. As a result, most analysts agree that we are closer to breaking our Army today than at any other time in its thirty-year history as an all-volunteer force.

For our national security, we will protect our country and our citizens by having a military that is second to none, by acting in ways that earn America respect in the world, by sharing burdens, using strong public diplomacy, and investing in the economic power of the American people, on whose strength our military might depends.

The Conservative Legacy

Damn the Facts, Full Speed Ahead. Conservatives live in a fantasy world, trying to twist reality to fit their expansionist theories rather than build policies that reflect the real world. In twisting facts, silencing critics and making preemptive war their preferred option, they have alienated the world and given energy and inspiration to those who hate America.

The president has embarked on a major war on the basis of intelligence that was consciously manipulated and consistently misread. In the rush to war, preparations for postwar occupation were ignored, critics were silenced and attacked, and ideology and wishful thinking were given precedence over planning and logic. The failure to secure postwar Iraq has created a rallying point and training ground for jihadists across the globe. The government's inability to provide meaningful reconstruction of Iraq, and new economic opportunities for Iraqis, has only reinforced the notion that America does not care about real democratic reform and human advancement in the Middle East. Three years after

September 11, terrorist attacks are increasing worldwide and al-Qaeda is once again on the rise.

Homeland Insecurity. Right-wing policies have made America less safe. A misguided war incites terrorists and diverts resources that could be used to make the American homeland safer. Aging Soviet nuclear weapons are working their way toward the black market and terrorist hands, while dictators in Iran and North Korea, knowing that we are tied down by the ill-planned Iraq war, act with impunity.

America's preparedness for future terrorist attacks remains woefully inadequate. Right now, the federal government is spending more to defend Iraq than it is to defend America. While cockpit doors, luggage screening, and passenger checkpoints have been strengthened, less than 5 percent of cargo placed on passenger aircraft is physically screened.[12] Our ports remain extraordinarily vulnerable. Only 5 percent of all shipping containers are inspected, despite estimates by security experts that it is only a matter of time before terrorists use a container to smuggle in a radiological device ("dirty bomb").[13] Many chemical plants and nuclear facilities remain vulnerable to terrorist infiltration and attack.

As both the 9/11 Commission and the CIA have concluded, American security continues to suffer from tremendous resource and knowledge gaps and disorganization in our intelligence operations. Interagency communication failures, inadequate human resources and intelligence contacts, and staid bureaucratic cultures hamper our ability to uncover and disrupt terrorist activities.

The blinkered focus on Iraq has diverted attention and resources away from other urgent challenges. More than a decade after the end of the Cold War, the United States and its allies still have not secured tens of thousands of loose nuclear weapons and deadly nuclear materials in the former Soviet Union—weapons likely to end up on the black market and in the hands of terrorists. Experts across the ideological spectrum agree that a major attack in the United States in the near term is possible and even probable.

Record Imports, Exporting Jobs. Conservatives send American jobs overseas to cut costs and bring foreign workers into the United States to undercut wages at home as core trade strategy.

The impact of the conservative economic agenda on both American and foreign workers has been devastating. The "Wal-Mart economy" favored by the right-wing leadership threatens to derail the American Dream and further erode living and working standards in other countries. At home, high-quality jobs are scarce, wages are stagnant, and benefits are on the decline as prices for such basic living necessities as housing, education, and health care have skyrocketed. American workers must compete with workers in other countries who receive low wages and no benefits.

Internationally, global trade has yet to yield sustainable benefits for a majority of the world's poorest countries. Low-income countries account for only three cents of every dollar generated through exports in the international trading system, and although 45 percent of America's exports are to the developing world, our investments in those markets are paltry.[14] Less than 1 percent of the total global flow of foreign direct investment is going to the world's least-developed countries.[15]

A Progressive Agenda

Moral Leadership and Multilateral Action. America must lead the global effort to secure freedom, democracy, human rights, and economic opportunities across the globe with moral as well as military strength.

- *Restore America's moral authority in global affairs.* Progressives must not shy away from the internationalism and democracy building that defined earlier progressive eras. This includes strong efforts to enlist our allies and lead global efforts to fight terrorism through direct action, through more cooperative intelligence arrangements, and through combined efforts to fight the conditions that breed terrorism in the first place—political repression, religious extremism, abject poverty, and the lack of economic opportunities.
- *Revamp American foreign assistance.* In a world rife with tensions—between the world's most powerful and powerless nations, between democracy and authoritarianism, between vast technological innovation and grotesque deprivation—America has both the opportunity and obligation to lead. Progressives should push for new U.S foreign assistance legislation, including the creation of a

single Department for International Development Cooperation, under which the current myriad of foreign aid programs would be consolidated; a new development policy focus to ensure support for the emergence of capable, democratic states; and reinvigorated global trade negotiations to enhance market dynamism. Our own prosperity and moral position in the world will be enhanced by fostering and supporting a world that is comprised of capable states, functioning economies, and healthy producers and consumers.

Integrated Global and Homeland Security. The fight against global terrorism and the proliferation of nuclear, biological, and chemical weapons requires unprecedented international cooperation and work at home. Efforts to protect ourselves cannot, and should not, be separated from those efforts abroad.

- *Stop the threat of catastrophic nuclear terrorism and nuclear proliferation.* In terms of policy imperatives, the continued proliferation of weapons of mass destruction across the globe, combined with the ongoing threat of fundamentalism and political extremism in the Middle East, poses the most pressing national security challenge facing America today. The U.S. response to this danger should be to secure nuclear weapons and materials everywhere they exist, improve homeland security protections here at home, and thoroughly restructure and reform our intelligence capabilities. We must not let the ongoing war in Iraq, as serious as it is, distract us from facing the real threat of a catastrophic terrorist attack and from developing plans to disrupt such an attack. This must be our nation's overriding national security priority.
- *Formulate a comprehensive approach to homeland security.* Terrorism is a global challenge, blurring the lines between domestic and international policies. This means we need a single strategy, unified structure, and comprehensive budget to properly integrate defense, homeland security, intelligence, law enforcement, and other programs directed against the terrorist threat. Washington must provide the leadership, coordination, and resources to make the United States safer, coordinating the contributions of communities, cities, states, and the private sector. Federal responsibility for homeland security cannot be outsourced.

- *Maintain transparency and openness in homeland security.* The government must be forthcoming in providing more information on threats and risks to the American people. The impulse of our leaders must be to share, not to hide or compartmentalize, information. Leadership that levels with the American people is pivotal to maintaining an open society—a pillar of American strength—as is finding the balance between protecting our borders and bringing in visitors, students, immigrants, and trading partners who promote the international understanding, cooperation, and opportunity that is crucial to reducing terrorism's appeal.

Save the All-Volunteer Army. Since September 11, 2001, the Army has been called upon to assume greater and broader responsibility than ever before. Our soldiers are needed to battle terrorism around the globe, protect the American homeland, and engage in peacekeeping, stabilization, and nation-building operations. Few imagined that the all-volunteer Army would be used in such a manner when it was designed thirty years ago, and the Bush administration has failed to make the appropriate changes to reflect the new environment. As a result, the active-duty Army is not large enough nor does it have the mix of skills necessary to meet current needs, and the reserve component is being used at unsustainable levels.[16]

- *Increase the size of the total Army by at least 86,000 troops.* The Army is overstretched and does not have sufficient numbers of active-duty troops trained for nontraditional duties such as nation building. The additional 86,000 troops should be added while maintaining the same quality standards that the Army has followed for the past five years, namely that at least 90 percent of all recruits have a high school diploma and 98 percent score average or above average on the Armed Forces Qualification Test. We should add two division-sized peacekeeping or stabilization units, double the size of the active-duty Special Forces, and add 10,000 military police, civil affairs specialists, engineers, and medical personnel to the active-duty force.
- *Amend "backdoor draft" policies and change stop-loss policy implementation.* To accomplish this, progressives should advocate legislation to reduce the length of the military service obligation—which by law lasts eight years from the date of initial

enlistment—to six years after enlistment or four years of active duty, whichever comes first. This change would prevent the men and women of the Individual Ready Reserve, who have already volunteered time to serve their country, from having their lives interrupted unfairly after they have completed their active-duty service. Additionally, we should work to change stop-loss policy implementation so that, as a matter of equity, no person is subject to stop-loss on more than one occasion without his or her consent. Enlisted people who are affected by stop-loss or whose tours in Iraq or Afghanistan are extended beyond one year should receive a bonus of $2,000 a month for the duration of their extra service.

- *Address quality-of-life issues to improve personnel readiness in both active-duty and selected-reserve units.* Progressives should support congressional legislation that would allow members of the Selected Reserve to enroll themselves and their families in the military's healthcare system, known as TRICARE. Enrollment in the TRICARE system would prevent reservists and their families from having to change healthcare plans when they are activated. Progressives should also take steps to maintain quality-of-life benefits such as special pay, commissaries, and schools on military bases.

- *Repeal the "Don't ask, don't tell" policy.* Progressives should advocate for the repeal of the "Don't ask, don't tell" policy that prohibits openly gay men and women from remaining in the armed services. That policy is counterproductive to military readiness. Nearly 10,000 people have been discharged because of "Don't ask, don't tell" over the past ten years. A significant number of them had expertise in areas in which the military has had personnel shortfalls, forcing the activation of individuals from the Individual Ready Reserve.

Free and Fair Trade. Improved living and working conditions in America require a properly functioning global economy and free and fair international trade.[17]

- *Adapt the global trading system to better reflect global aspirations and long-term prosperity.* A genuinely free *and* fair trading system is one that gives developing countries a seat at the negotiating table—not only because it is the right thing to do but also because talking among ourselves will never lead to expanding markets and new consumers for our goods.

- *Ensure that human rights, the rule of law, and labor and environmental standards are enshrined in a free and fair trade agenda.* It is possible to maintain both national sovereignty and corporate efficiency while standing up for basic principles that define us as progressives and democratic citizens.

- *Develop policy coherence between and among the international institutions charged with leading global development efforts—the IMF, World Bank, World Trade Organization, International Labor Organization, and United Nations.* As the growing acceptance of the UN's Millennium Development Goals and cooperative efforts on the Global Fund to Fight AIDS, Tuberculosis, and Malaria have demonstrated, it is possible to bring together public agencies and private nongovernmental organizations around strong, clear ideas.

Goal Three: Reforming the Political System

Progressives believe the privileges of American life for all must be accompanied by responsibilities from all and a genuine commitment to serve the larger community: citizens owe something to their families and localities; public officials to the national interest; and corporate leaders to shareholders, employees, consumers, and communities. Progressives recognize the responsibility to use the commonwealth for the common good and believe Americans have a duty to manage wisely the national and natural assets we hold in trust for future generations.

Rather than demanding accountability from all, lobbyists and private interests are corrupting the democratic process more than ever; public officials are not held accountable when their policies end in failure—in this administration, they are promoted; corporations give executives more pay and privileges while workers are downsized and their jobs go overseas; and military leaders are absolved when they send troops into battle without adequate plans or supplies.

For all sectors of society, we will insist on reform, responsibility, and accountability; we will protect the public trust and the public interest by ending cronyism, favoritism, and corruption in government and the private sector.

The Conservative Legacy

Government of the Special Interests, by the Special Interests, and for the Special Interests. A shadow government hidden from citizens' eyes makes federal policy based on special interest donations and lobbyists' legislative language. Their arrogance of power knows no bounds, whether it is Dick Cheney making backroom energy policy based on secret meetings with industry representatives or Tom DeLay taking $70,000 vacations on foreign agents' tabs—and then stacking the Ethics Committee to prevent an investigation.

Right-wing leaders have essentially turned the government over to high-powered lobbyists (many of them former political leaders themselves) and their self-interested corporate benefactors in the oil and gas, pharmaceutical, mining, insurance, and healthcare industries. The cozy partnership between corporate barons and right-wing leadership has grown so severe that the bipartisan House Ethics Committee has rebuked the House Majority Leader Tom DeLay (R-Texas) three times. In response, DeLay stripped the Ethics Committee of any real power to enforce the rules. Meanwhile, DeLay has been indicted on money-laundering charges, and his Texans for a Republican Majority political action committee is the subject of a grand jury investigation.

Profiting from Our Losses. Right-wing leaders take marching orders from campaign contributors as they systematically gut laws and regulations that protect the health and safety of average Americans. As argued in a joint report by the Center for American Progress and OMB Watch:

> Special interests have launched a sweeping assault on protections for public health, safety, the environment, and corporate responsibility—and unfortunately the Bush administration has given way. Crucial safeguards have been swept aside or watered down; emerging problems are being ignored; and enforcement efforts have been curtailed, threatening to render existing standards meaningless.
>
> This agenda puts special interests above the public interest, sacrificing a safer, healthier, more just America at the behest of industry lobbyists, corporate campaign contributors, and professional ideologues—many of whom the president has appointed to "regulate" the very interests they used to represent. . . .

. . . Every year, more than 40,000 people die on our nation's highways. Foodborne illnesses kill an estimated 7,000 and sicken 76 million. Nearly 6,000 workers die as a result of injury on the job, with an additional 50,000 to 60,000 killed by occupational disease. And asthma—linked to air pollution—is rising dramatically, afflicting 17 million, including six million children.[18]

A Return to the Roaring '20s. While the Right works to gut regulation, it also works to cut business taxes, all in the name of job creation. But billions in giveaways haven't given the American worker a break, and unemployment is still higher than it was when Bush took office.

The tax cut frenzy of the past four years has produced a monumental fiscal crisis in federal budgeting. The federal government has turned a projected $5.6 trillion budget surplus into a $2.3 trillion projected deficit over the next ten years—a downward shift of nearly $8 trillion in the nation's fiscal condition. For 2004 alone, the projected *surplus* of $397 billion has been replaced by a projected *deficit* of $422 billion—a downward swing of $819 billion in one year. Massive spending increases, the removal of sound fiscal constraints, and unaffordable tax cuts have left the nation's finances in tatters.

Deficits are a concern to many because of the negative impact large and persistent deficits might have on the economy in the long run. Deficits can lead to lower national savings and thus lower levels of output in the future. With the personal saving rate under 2 percent, it is even more troubling that the federal government is running up massive amounts of debt. In addition, with a large share of federal debt in the hands of foreign governments, large deficits raise potential concerns in the international finance and trade arena. Despite claims that we are "on track" to cut the deficit in half by 2008, the deficit has only gotten worse over the past several years.

In short, we are on an unsustainable path. Current policy will eventually have to be altered to correct for the imbalance between outlays and revenues, and choices must be made about how best to change course. Unfortunately, the president's budget continues the trend of additional tax reductions that benefit the wealthy, while placing an unfair share of the deficit reduction burden on the middle class.

Perhaps the most important concern with the deficit is that we are leaving a massive amount of debt to future generations and not responsibly addressing longer-term imbalances in the system. For example, as stated earlier, the revenue lost from the 2001–2003 tax cuts is triple the amount that would have made the Social Security system solvent for the next seventy-five years.

A Progressive Agenda

Give the American Government Back to the American People. As Al From and Bruce Reed of the Progressive Policy Institute and others have argued, progressives should once again claim the mantle of reform.[19]

- *Ensure transparency and really clean "House."* Ideas from Reed and others include: make the lobbying system transparent to the American people by posting the names, dates, and topics of meetings on the web as Congress debates, not after legislation is passed; shut the lobbying revolving door that encourages officials to cozy up to special interests by pushing a much longer ban on government officials becoming registered lobbyists after leaving government service; and enforce Congressional ethics with a real independent ethics committee, made up of retired members of Congress or even ordinary citizens immune to political pressures.

Fiscal Responsibility and Sound Budgets. Progressives must highlight how conservative stewardship is undermining America's economic strength. Fiscal mismanagement affects everyone. We must raise the stakes for Americans and promote sound fiscal and budget policies.

- *Restore PAYGO regulations and caps for discretionary spending.* For most of the 1990s, the pay-as-you-go, or PAYGO, rules required that if Congress wanted to cut a tax or create or expand an entitlement program, lawmakers had to offset the costs by raising other taxes or cutting other entitlement programs. The PAYGO rules were widely credited with imposing needed discipline while giving Congress the flexibility to make tax and spending changes that it deemed necessary. The rules expired several years ago and should be restored. Similarly, for most of the 1990s, Congress set annual limits, or caps, on total discretionary spending—programs from defense to education to transportation that it funds each year through the appropriations process. These caps enabled Congress to impose overall discipline while making choices and should be restored.

- *Create a commission to recommend eliminating ineffective programs.* Modeled on the successful military base-closing commissions of recent years, a program-closing commission would give Congress a list of programs to consider in an all-or-nothing, up-or-down vote. A commission could give lawmakers the political freedom to make tough choices about ineffective programs.

- *Improve the accuracy of the Consumer Price Index and apply the savings in tax and spending programs to deficit reduction.* Many experts believe that the CPI overstates inflation. However, the CPI is the measure that the federal government uses to calculate increases in many federal benefit programs as well as the tax code. A reformed CPI that would more accurately measure inflation would protect the income standards of average Americans who receive benefits while providing budget savings to reduce the deficit.

Energy Independence. Progressives must rethink national energy policy and take a cue from the innovative solutions for energy independence outlined by the Apollo Project and the Energy Future Coalition to cut our dependence on foreign oil, stop handouts to polluters, help create millions of new jobs, and clean up our air and water.

- *Set a national energy agenda that will protect our national security, strengthen our economy and create jobs, and preserve the health of the world and its people for generations to come.* America now has the technologies necessary to dramatically improve energy self-sufficiency, but we need the will to use them. Progressives should push for a national energy plan that transitions away from oil dependence, enhances domestic energy supply, prioritizes energy efficiency to enhance supply and improve reliability, and tackles global warming. We should diversify our domestic energy use, promote bio-fuels and new types of automotive technology, and modernize our energy plants with cleaner technology. The private sector is already experimenting with many of these ideas for innovative and profitable solutions to long-term energy needs.

Increase Innovation in Government. In order to handle public needs in the twenty-first century, the government must adopt the mentality of innovation and embrace technology as a means to better and more efficient policy and regulatory development.

- *Give the government the tools it needs to improve our lives.* Progressives should push to modernize data collection to address critical gaps in our knowledge of policy effectiveness, integrate data management and dissemination across federal agencies, and analyze data to assess what is and is not working. The goal is to create more effective public safeguards for a cleaner environment and safer, healthier communities. The free-market system alone will never adequately address these issues, and progressives should push for revitalized consumer protections and greater public health and safety measures.

WHAT PROGRESSIVES STAND FOR

As commentators continue to reflect on the 2004 national elections and assess the state of American politics today, they invariably ask: "What do progressives stand for?" The fact that they ask this question reveals the imbalance of modern political discourse and the total dominion of the conservative intellectual, partisan, and media infrastructure over alternative viewpoints. More than anything, however, this question highlights the failure of progressives to capture the public's imagination. This is our fault and our fault alone.

Progressives have allowed the ideals and ideas behind America's crowning social and economic achievements to be reduced—through outside agitation and self-inflicted negligence—to a conservative punch line and historical footnote. If Americans fail to understand progressive ideas for making the country a safer and better place to live, work, and raise a family, it is because our side has failed to make the case for core progressive values.

We have taken this challenge to heart in trying to articulate a progressive message, grounded in principles and responsive to America's position in the twenty-first century. We claim no monopoly on truth in presenting our principles and policy agenda. We merely aim to bring forth the proud progressive tradition of responding to great national needs with an equally strong public spirit and commitment to social and political change.

NOTES

The authors would like to thank the staff of the Center for American Progress for their expertise in producing the Progressive Priorities policy series featured throughout this chapter and to David Dreyer, Charles Sweeney, and Eric London for their editorial help in finalizing the chapter.

1. See Herbert Croly's 1909 classic, *The Promise of American Life* (New York: Capricorn Books, 1964), and Teddy Roosevelt's 1910 "New Nationalism" speech from Osawatomie, Kansas.
2. John Judis, "Structural Flaw," *New Republic*, February 28, 2005.
3. Richard Kogan and Robert Greenstein, "President Portrays Social Security Shortfall as Enormous, but His Tax Cuts and Drug Benefit Will Cost at Least Five Times as Much," Center on Budget and Policy Priorities, revised February 11, 2005, available at http://www.cbpp.org/1-4-05socsec.htm.
4. The $427 billion estimate from the 2006 *Budget of the U.S. Government* does not include the full cost of a supplemental budget request expected to cover the military operations in Iraq and Afghanistan.
5. For a complete listing of the proposed budget cuts, see the Center for American Progress, "Making the Wrong Choices: An Analysis of the President's 2006 Budget," February 2005, available at http://www.americanprogress.org/atf/cf/{E9245FE4-9A2B-43C7-A521-5D6FF2E06E03}/Wrong%20Choices%20An%20Analysis%20of%20the%202006%20Budget.pdf.
6. Center for American Progress, "Wrong Choices."
7. Jack Hadley and John Holahan, "The Cost of Care for the Uninsured: What Do We Spend, Who Pays, and What Would Full Coverage Add to Medical Spending?" Kaiser Commission on Medicaid and the Uninsured, May 2004, available at http://www.kff.org/uninsured/upload/The-Cost-of-Care-for-the-Uninsured-What-Do-We-Spend-Who-Pays-and-What-Would-Full-Coverage-Add-to-Medical-Spending.pdf.
8. Institute of Medicine, *Hidden Costs, Value Lost: Uninsurance in America* (Washington: National Academies Press, 2003).
9. Leonard E. Burman, William Gale, Jeffrey Rohaly, and Matthew Hall, "Key Points on the Alternative Minimum Tax," Urban-Brookings Tax Policy

Center, January 2004, available at http://www.brookings.edu/views/op-ed/
gale/20040121amt.htm.

10. U.S. Congress, Joint Economic Committee, "The Alternative Minimum
Tax for Individuals: A Growing Burden," May 2001, available at http://www
.house.gov/jec/tax/amt.pdf.

11. Sen. John McCain (R-Ariz.), for example, explained in proposing a Corporate Welfare Commission: "There are more than 100 corporate subsidy programs in the federal budget today, requiring the federal government to spend
approximately $65 billion a year. Terminating even some of these programs
could save taxpayers tens of billions of dollars each year" (press release, April
17, 2002).

12. Testimony of Norman J. Rabkin, General Accounting Office (GAO), before the U.S. Senate Subcommittee on Aviation of the Committee on Com-
merce, Science, and Transportation, March 30, 2004.

13. Graham Allison, *Nuclear Terrorism: The Ultimate Preventable Catastro-
phe* (New York: Times Books/Henry Holt, 2004), 8.

14. Kevin Watkins and Penny Fowler, *Rigged Rules and Double Standards:
Trade, Globalisation, and the Fight against Poverty* (Oxford, England: Oxfam,
2002), 7–8.

15. "Foreign Direct Investment on the Rise in World's Poorest Countries,"
UN News Centre, May 10, 2001, available at http://www.un.org/apps/news/
storyAr.asp?NewsID=1056&Cr=poor&Cr1=.

16. Mark Mazzetti, "U.S. Military Is Stretched Too Thin, Defense Board
Warns," *Los Angeles Times*, September 30, 2004; Hearing of the National Se-
curity, Emerging Threats, and International Relations Subcommittee of the
House Government Reform Committee, April 29, 2003.

17. John Podesta and Sonal Shah, "A Progressive Trade Agenda," Center for
American Progress, May 20, 2004, available at http://www.americanprogress
.org/site/pp.asp?c=biJRJ8OVF&b=80308.

18. Reece Rushing, "Special Interest Takeover: The Bush Administration
and the Dismantling of Public Safeguards," Center for American Progress and
OMB Watch, May 2004, 7, available at http://www.americanprogress.org/atf/
cf/%7be9245fe4-9a2b-43c7-a521-5d6ff2e06e03%7d/sispecialinterests.pdf.

19. Al From and Bruce Reed, "What We Stand For: Americans Don't Know
What Democrats Believe In; It's Time to Tell Them," *Blueprint* 2005, no. 1
(March 16, 2005), available at http://www.ndol.org/ndol_ci.cfm?kaid=127&
subid=171&contentid=253206.

7

CLOSING THE 527 LOOPHOLE

Craig Holman

With enormous fanfare and expectations, Congress adopted in 2002—
and the U.S. Supreme Court approved—the nation's most sweeping reforms to the Federal Election Campaign Act (FECA) in nearly a
quarter-century. Officially titled the Bipartisan Campaign Reform Act
(BCRA) of 2002, and widely known as the McCain-Feingold Act after
its principal Senate sponsors, the new reforms sought to salvage the contribution limits of the fledgling federal election law.

McCain-Feingold's primary objective is to save the contribution limits on wealthy individuals and the ban on campaign money from corporations and labor unions that comprise the essence of federal campaign
finance laws. The new law reaffirms the ban on "soft money"—funds
raised in excess of the contribution limits from wealthy individuals or
from corporations and unions. It explicitly prohibits federal officeholders, candidates, and the parties from raising or spending soft money in
federal elections. But the law itself does not explicitly address "independent" political organizations, especially Section 527 political organizations, which operate outside the scope of federal election law.

Section 527 organizations make no campaign contributions, and so
they need not register as political action committees with the Federal
Election Commission (FEC). They effectively sidestep most federal

election restrictions on fund-raising by avoiding any of the eight so-
called magic words in their advertising—such as "vote for," "elect," or
"defeat"—that the Supreme Court in the 1976 *Buckley v. Valeo* decision
listed as a test of whether an advertisement is a campaign ad subject to
campaign finance regulation.[1] These organizations register only with the
Internal Revenue Service under Section 527 of the tax code, declaring
to the IRS that their primary purpose is to affect elections, and thus are
awarded special tax advantages. But their election activities remain immune from federal contribution limits and soft money prohibitions.[2]

Section 527 has quickly turned into a major loophole of federal campaign finance law, already endangering the brand new achievements of
McCain-Feingold. "Independent" Section 527 groups, such as the Swift
Boat Veterans for Truth on the Republican side and the George
Soros–financed Media Fund on the Democratic side, had as their sole
purpose affecting the outcome of the 2004 presidential election, yet operated outside most campaign finance restrictions that applied to all
other players in the election, able to raise and spend unlimited money
that would otherwise be illegal in federal elections.

Democratic-leaning Section 527 groups first tapped into this loophole, making it appear that progressive electoral interests would be well
served by maintaining it. But Republican-leaning groups quickly recognized how Section 527 could be exploited to the full advantage of
George Bush. In the final weeks of the 2004 presidential campaign, Republican Section 527 groups outspent Democratic groups 3 to 1 and
played a decisive role in throwing the election to Bush. As we have seen
over and over again, clever Democrats often are the first to poke a hole
in the dam of campaign finance law, only to see wealthy Republicans
jump in and fully exploit it. If money is to be unregulated and unlimited
in elections, the wealthy will enjoy a decisive advantage. This works to
the disadvantage of progressives.

Reforms that limit contributions to Section 527s as they are limited to
political action committees (PACs) are justified by: the rapid growth of
527 groups since the political party soft money system was shut down by
McCain-Feingold; the type of activities performed by and the significant influence of these groups; and the exceptional concentration of
wealthy special interests funding them. Democrats should advocate
closing the Section 527 loophole as part of a broad agenda of govern-

ment reform. It is good politics for progressives—and it is good policy. This chapter will explain why, by examining the conditions that led to the collapse of federal campaign finance law, its recovery by McCain-Feingold, and the subsequent political battles that have worked to the benefit of conservative interests.

THE TWIN PILLARS OF MCCAIN-FEINGOLD

McCain-Feingold was signed by the president and enacted on March 27, 2002. It sought to achieve two principal objectives: (1) a ban on soft money used by federal officeholders, candidates, and parties in federal elections, and (2) a redefinition of campaign advertisements subject to the Federal Election Campaign Act to include "electioneering communications" as well as express advocacy. "Electioneering communications" are defined as any broadcast advertisement that depicts a federal candidate and targets that candidate's voting constituency within thirty days of a primary election or sixty days of a general election.

Soft Money

The concept of "soft money," created and enshrined in federal regulations by the Federal Election Commission, had rendered federal contribution limits virtually meaningless by the 2000 federal elections.[3] Even though corporations and labor unions have been prohibited from using their treasury funds to affect federal elections for about fifty years,[4] and individuals have faced a $1,000 per election contribution limit since the amendment of FECA in 1974,[5] all of these entities pumped into federal elections as much money as they wished through the FEC's soft-money loophole.

In the legal challenge to FECA, the Supreme Court in the *Buckley* decision narrowed the application of federal election law by parties and independent groups to activities that "expressly advocate" the election or defeat of federal candidates. In the infamous footnote 52 of the *Buckley* decision, the court gave eight examples of words that, used in advertising, would distinguish campaign ads, which are subject to FECA regulation, from issue ads, which are not. Known as the "magic words" standard, ads that used such words as "vote for," "elect," or "defeat" were classified by the court as campaign advertising subject to the limits and prohibitions of federal election law.

The Federal Election Commission took the express advocacy distinction and expanded it into a gaping loophole in the law. The FEC determined that "soft money"—money from corporate and union treasuries and in excess of the contribution limits from individuals—could be used by parties and independent groups in part to pay for issue ads as well as for nonfederal election activity, such as influencing state elections or mobilizing voters. The elections agency developed regulations applying an "allocation ratio" detailing how much soft money versus "hard money" (funds raised from individuals within the contribution limits) could be used by party committees to finance these types of ads in the late 1980s.[6] A similar allocation ratio applied to PACs registered with the FEC for the purpose of making campaign contributions to federal candidates. This regulatory decision allowed unlimited funds from corporations, unions, and wealthy individuals to finance all types of election activities, including expensive television advertising targeting federal candidates but steering clear of using any of the eight magic words.[7]

By the 2000 federal elections, the contribution limits and source prohibitions on money in federal elections had all but collapsed because of the soft-money loophole and the use of electioneering issue advocacy. Then came McCain-Feingold.

Title I of the McCain-Feingold Act reaffirms the ban on soft money in federal elections. National party committees are explicitly prohibited from raising or spending soft money for any purpose. This ban applies to any entity that is established or controlled by a national party committee. Just as importantly, McCain-Feingold prohibits federal officeholders or candidates from raising or spending soft money in connection to federal election activity, including a ban on soliciting soft money for other groups, except for limited activities of nonprofit groups. Federal officeholders and candidates may not raise or spend soft money for state and local candidates and parties,[8] although they may raise up to $20,000 in soft money from individuals specifically for the voter mobilization activities of each Section 527 or 501(c) nonprofit group. Officeholders and candidates may raise unlimited soft money for 501(c) nonprofit groups so long as the funds are not used in connection with federal election activity.

"Federal election activity" is defined rather broadly as any advertisement that promotes or attacks a federal candidate, generic party campaign activity, voter mobilization activity in general, and voter registration drives within 120 days of a federal election. As a general rule, if federal candidates are on the ballot, activity affecting that election is classified as federal election activity and cannot be financed using soft money by federal officeholders, candidates, parties, or PACs. FEC regulations, however, continue to exempt nonprofit groups from the soft-money ban as it relates to federal election activity, except in the case of electioneering communications.

Electioneering Communications

The "electioneering communications" provision of McCain-Feingold expands the class of advertisements subject to regulation because they are defined as campaign ads rather than issue ads. In addition to the magic-words standard of express advocacy, any broadcast ad that refers to a clearly identified federal candidate within sixty days of a general election or thirty days of a primary election, and which targets that candidate's constituency, is also classified as a campaign advertisement. An ad is considered targeted to a candidate's constituency if it can be received by 50,000 or more persons in the candidate's district (as determined by the Federal Communications Commission). "Broadcast ads" include television, radio, cable, and satellite advertisements, but not Internet advertisements. Electioneering communications and express advocacy communications must be paid for with hard money and the source of funds and expenditures disclosed to the FEC.

One key omission in the law regarding electioneering communications is that McCain-Feingold allows these ads to be financed with unlimited contributions from wealthy individuals. The largest bulk of soft money that went to the parties to finance these types of ads came directly from corporate and union treasuries. Of the top ten soft-money donors to the national Democratic Party in the 2000 election, eight were labor unions and two were corporations. Of the top ten soft-money donors to the national Republican Party that same election cycle, eight were corporations, one was the National Rifle Association, and one was the Republican Party of California. None of the top ten soft-money donors to the parties were wealthy individuals.[9]

In banning soft money to pay for electioneering communications, the drafters of McCain-Feingold placed that specific provision in the section of federal election law that bars only corporate and union contributions, not contributions in excess of the limits from individuals.[10] Federal officeholders and parties cannot raise or spend any soft money in federal elections, but outside groups that finance electioneering communications immediately before an election, including Section 527 groups, may use unlimited funds raised from individuals to pay for these ads and must report the sources of funds and expenditures within twenty-four hours to the FEC. Thus, while officeholders and parties are banned from using any soft money to pay for these ads, outside groups are restricted from using only two of the three sources of soft money to pay for electioneering communications.

THE COURT EXPANDS THE LAW, BUT THE FEC BALKS

The scope of the McCain-Feingold reforms was extended even further by the Supreme Court in its review of the law. The court upheld nearly every aspect of the law in its expedited 2003 decision, *McConnell v. FEC*,[11] and even admonished the Federal Election Commission for letting money in politics get so out of hand. FEC regulations, noted the court, created the problem of soft money. In the words of the justices, "The FEC regulations permitted more than Congress, in enacting FECA, had ever intended."[12]

Just as importantly, the court chided the FEC and others for taking the examples of "magic words" in footnote 52 of the *Buckley* decision too literally, understanding the eight words as *examples* of express advocacy, not as an *exclusive description* of it.[13] In scaling back the magic-words standard for defining campaign advertising, the *McConnell* decision opened the door for reestablishing a broader definition of federal election activities subject to regulation under FECA and McCain-Feingold. Suddenly, whole classes of activity that the FEC ruled fell outside the scope of regulation were again captured under federal election law as interpreted by the court.

But the court's opinion was not enough to move the FEC on the issue. After months of reevaluating its regulations permitting the soft-money loophole in 2004, the FEC declined to repeal or significantly modify its soft-money regulations. The FEC's inaction put the ball back into Congress's court, where legislation was pending in 2005 to classify Section 527 political organizations involved in federal elections as "political committees" subject to the requirements of federal election law.[14]

USING THE TAX CODE TO CIRCUMVENT
FEDERAL ELECTION LAW

Section 527 of the tax code was not originally designed as a means for political operatives to evade the contribution limits and disclosure requirements of federal election laws. It was part of the post-Watergate reform movement. In order to shield campaign contributions from taxation, Congress developed a unique provision of the tax code (Section 527) for party and candidate committees to register their nontaxable campaign contributions. Since party and candidate committees were also specifically subject to FECA requirements, Section 527 was not used as a loophole by these committees.

Two decades later, however, the Sierra Club realized that Section 527 of the tax code could be used to avoid contribution limits and reporting requirements, as long as the group did not make campaign contributions or use express advocacy in its political advertisements. The Sierra Club was soon followed by dozens, and eventually hundreds, of other nonprofit groups. Unlike 501(c) nonprofit groups, Section 527 political organizations declare that their primary purpose is to affect elections, but not in a fashion that would be captured by FECA. These political "stealth PACs" mushroomed in number and spending activity.

In the 2000 presidential primary election, which featured a heated campaign for the Republican nomination between George Bush and John McCain, one stealth PAC called "Republicans for Clean Air" ran a series of ads depicting John McCain as a friend of polluting coal-burning power plants and ending with the slogan: "Bush: Leading so each day dawns brighter." The true identity of the group sponsoring the ad evaded the press and public for some time, until the sponsors—Sam and Charles Wyly, two millionaire friends of George Bush—called a press conference to boast of their handiwork. A slightly chagrined Congress responded with a law in July 2000 requiring all 527s to file regular financial disclosure reports with the IRS.[15] The disclosure requirement was further strengthened by the Brady-Lieberman Section 527 disclosure law in 2002, but these groups still remain outside the source prohibitions and contribution limits of FECA.

That means Section 527 of the tax code holds the best of both worlds for political operatives who want to raise and spend unregulated money in federal elections. Section 527 groups are not hampered by the legal constraints against excessive political activity that apply to 501(c) nonprofit groups. And Section 527 groups are not hampered by the source prohibitions and contribution limits of FECA. When McCain-Feingold gave the ban on soft money under federal election law real teeth, its supporters expected that some of the soft money that had previously gone to party committees and federal officeholders would flow to these stealth PACs, but the extent of the migration surprised many observers and highlighted Section 527 groups as a major soft-money loophole.

SECTION 527 FINANCES IN THE 2004 ELECTION CYCLE

Since the mid-1990s, Section 527s have played an increasingly significant role in federal elections. In the 2002 election cycle, more than 19,900 Section 527 groups were registered with the Internal Revenue Service. Most of these groups, however, focused on state and local election activity. Only about two hundred of the registered Section 527s reported significant financial expenditures affecting federal elections.[16] Far fewer of these groups were devoted exclusively or primarily to affecting federal elections.

In the 2004 election cycle, federal Section 527 groups raised and spent 150 percent more than in 2002. As shown in table 7.1, money flowing to Section 527 groups increased from $151 million in the 2002 federal elections to $405 million in 2004—an increase of $254 million.

To be sure, this increase in Section 527 activity in 2004 represents an overall decline in soft-money spending in federal elections due to McCain-Feingold. The Campaign Finance Institute estimates that, in the 2002 election cycle, national and state parties in federal elections raised $591 million in soft money that is now banned under McCain-

**Table 7.1.   Overview of Federal Section 527
Political Organizations, 2002 and 2004 Election Cycles**

	2002 Election Cycle		2004 Election Cycle		
	Number of Groups	Total Receipts (billions)	Number of Groups	Organized after BCRA	Total Receipts (billions)
Democratic-Oriented Groups	28[a]	$107.2	59	41	$321.2
Republican-Oriented Groups	14[b]	43.7	21	9	83.9
All Groups	42	150.9	80	50	405.1

Source: Steve Weissman and Ruth Hassan, "BCRA and the 527 Groups," Campaign Finance Institute, draft chapter revised March 8, 2005, available at http://www.cfinst.org/studies/ElectionAfterReform/pdf/ EAR_527Chapter.pdf, from The Election after *Reform: Money, Politics and the Bipartisan Campaign Reform Act*, ed. Michael J. Malbin (Lanham, Md.: Rowman & Littlefield, forthcoming)
[a]Plus 26 leadership PACs (leadership PACs are committees established and controlled by officeholders; prior to BCRA, these PACs could raise and spend soft money)
[b]Plus 20 leadership PACs

Feingold.[17] Another $151 million was raised by federal 527 groups, for a total of $741 million in soft money. In the 2004 cycle, the political parties and federal officeholders were banned from raising soft money, but 527 groups raised $405 million, for an overall net reduction of $337 million in soft money from 2002 levels.

Nevertheless, if left unchecked, Section 527 organizations are likely to continue increasing their share of campaign finances in future elections and will probably eliminate any gains provided by McCain-Feingold. The 150-percent increase in funding for Section 527 groups in the course of a single election cycle is revealing enough of the potential for future growth. But the point is also driven home by the fact that most of the Section 527 groups in 2004 were newly organized and nearly half of the new money to Section 527 groups came from just 52 individuals.

Again, table 7.1 lists the number of federal Section 527 groups active in the 2004 elections. While eighty groups were exclusively or primarily involved in the 2004 federal elections, fifty of these groups—or 63 percent—were organized for the first time in the 2004 election cycle. A flurry of Section 527 groups were organized the last few days before McCain-Feingold became effective at the end of the 2002 elections, many on November 4, 2002. The FEC had earlier determined that it would not look into any sharing of staff or resources prior to the effective date of McCain-Feingold in judging whether the new groups are coordinated with other political parties or campaigns.

Very few people accounted for the influx of new soft money into Section 527 organizations, indicating how easy it is for a handful of financial angels—be they individuals, unions, or corporations—to have a tremendous impact on the scope of 527 activity. As shown in tables 7.2 and 7.3, twenty-four people gave $2 million or more in the 2004 election cycle to Section 527 groups, raising more than $142 million, or 35 percent of total funds raised. Another twenty-eight people gave $1 million or more to 527 groups in 2004, raising another $35 million. By comparison, in 2002 no individual gave $2 million or more to a 527 group, and only two individuals gave $1 million or more in that election cycle. Some fifty-two people—all of whom contributed at least $1 million—gave 44 percent of all money collected by federal 527 groups in 2004.

The dominant role of wealthy individuals providing the bulk of soft money to Section 527 groups also holds significant ramifications for the electioneering communications pillar of McCain-Feingold. When it comes to these outside groups, McCain-Feingold prohibits the use of only corporate and union money to pay for campaign ads that air within sixty days of a general election, not soft money raised from wealthy individuals. As a result, the ability of Section 527 groups to raise and spend

Table 7.2. Patterns of Individual Contributions to Federal Section 527 Groups, 2002 and 2004 Election Cycles

Range of Donations	Number of Donors	Total Amount	Percent of Funds from Individuals (%)
2002 Election Cycle			
$2,000,000 and above	0	—	0
$1,000,000 to $1,999,999	2	$2,152,000	6
$500,000 to $999,999	8	6,132,190	17
$250,000 to $499,999	13	4,238,550	11
$100,000 to $249,999	43	5,872,372	16
$5,000 to $99,999	1,165	18,672,941	50
2004 Election Cycle			
$2,000,000 and above	24	$142,497,241	56
$1,000,000 to $1,999,999	28	35,216,957	14
$500,000 to $999,999	25	16,380,500	6
$250,000 to $499,999	36	12,297,148	5
$100,000 to $249,999	152	20,360,946	8
$5,000 to $99,999	1,617	29,511,550	12

Source: Steve Weissman and Ruth Hassan, Campaign Finance Institute, February 9, 2005

Table 7.3. Top 24 Individual Donors to Federal Section 527 Organizations, 2004 Election Cycle

Rank	Contributor	Democratic-Oriented	Republican-Oriented	Total Contributions
1	George Soros Soros Fund Management	X		$24,000,000
2	Peter Lewis Peter B. Lewis/Progressive Corp.	X		$22,545,000
3	Steven Bing Shangri-La Entertainment	X		$13,902,682
4	Herb and Marion Sandler Golden West Financial	X		$13,007,959
5	Bob J. Perry Perry Homes		X	$8,060,000
6 (tie)	Alex Spanos AG Spanos Companies		X	$5,000,000
6 (tie)	Ted Waitt Gateway, Inc.	X		$5,000,000
6 (tie)	Dawn Arnall Ameriquest Capital		X	$5,000,000
9	T. Boone Pickens BP Capital		X	$4,600,000
10	Jerry Perenchio Chartwell Partners, LLC		X	$4,000,000
11	Andrew Rappaport August Capital	X		$3,858,400
12	Harold Simmons Contran Corp.		X	$3,700,000
13	Alida R. Messinger Alida Messinger Charitable Trust	X		$3,447,200
14	Jeffrey and Jeanne Levy-Hinte TippingPoint Technologies	X		$3,425,000
15	Linda Pritzker Sustainable World Corp.	X		$3,365,000
16	Fred Eychaner Newsweb Corp.	X		$3,075,000
17	Lewis Cullman Cullman Foundation	X		$2,651,000
18	Alice Walton Rocking W Ranch		X	$2,600,000
19	Carl Lindner American Financial Group		X	$2,225,000
20	Robert Glaser RealNetworks, Inc.	X		$2,229,000
21	Agnes Varis Agvar Chemicals	X		$2,006,000
22 (tie)	Terry Ragon Intersystems Corp.	X		$2,000,000
22 (tie)	Richard DeVos, Sr. Amway/Alticor, Inc.		X	$2,000,000
22 (tie)	Jay Van Andel Amway/Alticor, Inc.		X	$2,000,000
Total		14	10	$142,497,241

Source: Steve Weissman and Ruth Hassan, "BCRA and the 527 Groups," Campaign Finance Institute, draft chapter revised March 8, 2005, available at http://www.cfinst.org/studies/ElectionAfterReform/pdf/EAR_527Chapter.pdf, from *The Election after Reform: Money, Politics and the Bipartisan Campaign Reform Act,* ed. Michael J. Malbin (Lanham, Md.: Rowman & Littlefield, forthcoming)

soft money to pay for electioneering communications in 2004 largely went unimpeded. These groups could take corporate and union soft money to pay at any time for infrastructural development, including fund-raising, and direct mail and print ads and voter mobilization activities. The funds raised from wealthy individuals were then diverted into financing electioneering communications supporting or attacking federal candidates within sixty days of the general election.

Clearly the Section 527 loophole has become the playground for multimillionaires who want to select our officeholders. In the 2004 presidential election, there were a handful of progressive millionaires, such as George Soros, Peter Lewis, and Steven Bing, who jumped in first and made extensive use of this loophole. Many conservative wealthy individuals and corporations had initially shied away from the Section 527 route as the Republican Party challenged the legality of Section 527 groups, both in calling for the FEC to revise its prior regulations permitting the Section 527 loophole and in court during the 2004 elections. When the legal maneuvers did not succeed, Republicans decided to join in the Section 527 fundraising and spending frenzy with zeal late in the election cycle. In short order, Republican-leaning special interests exploited the loophole that had been the exclusive province of Democrats.

Because of their early advantage, Democratic-leaning Section 527 groups amassed an overall 4-to-1 dollar advantage over Republican-leaning Section 527 groups in the 2004 election cycle (see table 7.1). But this Democratic advantage appears to be spurious and is reminiscent of the pattern of soft-money fund-raising for the national parties, where Democrats led early, only to have Republicans swiftly catch up. As table

Table 7.4.   Broadcast Spending by Section 527 Political Organizations in the Final Three Weeks of the 2004 Presidential Election

Presidential 527 Organizations	Total Broadcast Expenditures
Democratic-Oriented	$10,276,499
Republican-Oriented	$29,736,863
All Groups	$40,013,362

Source: Alex Knott, Aron Pilhofer, and Derek Willis, "GOP 527s Outspend Dems in Late Ad Blitz: Progress for America and Swift Boats Dominated Airwaves in Swing States," Center for Public Integrity, November 3, 2004, available at http://www.publicintegrity.org/527/report.aspx?aid=421&sid=200

7.4 demonstrates, in the final three weeks of the 2004 elections, Republican Section 527 groups outspent Democratic groups by a margin of 3 to 1.

Republican constituencies, particularly the corporate world, may have been slow to recognize the value of the Section 527 soft-money loophole. But in the end, Republican money flowed into Section 527 groups, overwhelming Democratic money to these groups and undermining John Kerry's electoral prospects.

WHY DEMOCRATS DO NOT BENEFIT FROM THE SECTION 527 LOOPHOLE

The long-term impact of Section 527 groups on election outcomes is exceedingly difficult to measure because it varies from year to year and is influenced by the amount of money raised, the timing of Section 527 group efforts, and the legal constraints imposed at a given time by the law and the tax code. This variability should make progressives think carefully about how strongly they want to rely on the efforts of 527 groups, especially in light of how quickly and effectively Republican 527 groups emerged as a force on behalf of President Bush late in the 2004 campaign.

Furthermore, the contributions made by Democratic-leaning groups could, and arguably should, be coordinated under the umbrella of the Democratic Party. In 2004, Section 527 organizations participated in a wide range of election activities, including door-to-door canvassing, phone banks, newspaper ads, direct mail, and radio and television advertising. Closing the Section 527 loophole would mean the loss of these activities by independent groups, but this in turn would encourage the Democratic Party to develop and oversee these functions in-house, in the manner that the Republican Party runs its canvassing and turnout operation. The advantage to Democrats would be greater control over these critically important functions, which could give Democrats an organizational advantage now enjoyed by Republicans.

Although closing the loophole would mean the loss of advertising dollars and independently crafted messages from affiliated groups, it is not clear that this would pose a disadvantage to progressive causes. To understand

why, look at how Section 527 groups assisted the media campaigns of
the 2004 nominees. The Media Fund, America Coming Together
(ACT), the AFL-CIO, and MoveOn.org heavily hit the airwaves on behalf of Kerry, and their impact was most strongly felt between March
and August when Kerry became the Democrats' presumptive nominee
but still could not qualify for general election public financing until officially nominated at the Democratic convention. Since Bush was running unopposed, he was able to hoard funds to employ late in the primary season, when Kerry had exhausted his primary campaign budget,
but the influx of Democratic-leaning Section 527 spending late in the
primary season helped neutralize the Bush advantage.[18]

Without question, this gave Kerry an important tactical asset. But
consider the unusual circumstances necessary to place a Democratic
nominee-in-waiting at such an extreme disadvantage. In order for the
circumstances of 2004 to repeat themselves, a future election cycle
would have to produce an incumbent Republican president with no primary challengers running against a crowded field of Democrats engaged
in a long primary struggle with each other. To justify maintaining the
Section 527 loophole on the basis of the role played by affiliated groups
in keeping Kerry on the air in summer 2004—valuable as that effort
was—is to argue on narrow tactical grounds for an eventuality that may
not present itself again for years.

It also requires overlooking the full effect that Section 527 groups had
on the campaign. Although Democratic-leaning groups served a useful
purpose for the Kerry campaign by helping to neutralize the Bush attack
late in the primary election, Republican-leaning Section 527 groups
served an even more valuable purpose for the Bush campaign by taking
the burden of attacking Kerry's war record away from Bush, who without the 527 loophole would not have been able to ride above the fray
while surrogates criticized Kerry for his war record.

Republican Section 527s, which organized late in the election cycle, targeted their air campaign after the Democratic convention to
undermine Kerry's convention appeal as a war veteran. Just one ad by
Swift Boat Veterans for Truth was so sensational that it received
nearly as much newsplay as the advertising campaign itself. The initial Swift Boat Veterans advertising campaign was a fairly low-budget
affair of $600,000, largely footed by a single individual, Bob Perry, a

construction baron in Texas. After just the first airing of the ad, the news media picked it up and kept it on the airwaves as news for weeks. As news of Swift Boat Veterans spread, its campaign budget swelled. By the end of the campaign, Swift Boat Veterans was able to raise and spend about $28 million from corporate interests and wealthy individuals attacking John Kerry's candidacy, significantly outspending most of the Democratic-leaning Section 527 groups in the final weeks of the election.[19]

The Swift Boat spending was a decisive factor in the eventual outcome of the election. The campaigns of Swift Boat Veterans and another major Republican-leaning Section 527, Progress for America, proved very effective in reaching voters and raising serious doubts about the centerpiece of Kerry's campaign, his war record. In one panel study, about one in four undecided voters said they were less likely to vote for Kerry after viewing the Swift Boat ads.[20] In a telephone survey of likely voters, 76 percent of respondents were aware of the issues presented by the Swift Boat Veterans for Truth—an unprecedented voter retention rate for a campaign ad.[21] Progress for America's campaign salvo came later in the election cycle, featuring Bush as a compassionate leader through the eyes of a young woman who had lost her mother in the September 11, 2001, terrorist attacks. This positive message played well in concert with the negative attack ads against Kerry by the Swift Boat Veterans. All the while, President Bush could claim no direct involvement in the attack ads, permitting him to claim the politically valuable high ground while remaining immune from voter backlash against the negativity of the Swift Boat campaign.

PROGRESSIVES SHOULD WANT TO CLOSE THE LAST MAJOR SOFT-MONEY LOOPHOLE

The appropriate solution to the problem posed by 527 groups is not to keep in place a system of unlimited and unregulated campaign financing by outside groups, but to fix the presidential public financing system. In fact, fixing the presidential public financing system is the next priority for the campaign finance reform community after the problem of the Section 527 soft money loophole is resolved. A legislative model is already in the works, which encompasses several modifications to the public financing system, including:

- Promoting full participation by presidential candidates in the public financing system by appreciably increasing funding for an expanded program.
- Requiring presidential candidates at the outset of the primary election to opt in or out of the entire public financing program for both the primary and general elections. (Currently, candidates may opt out in the primary and jump back in during the general election.)
- Supplying additional public funds to participating candidates to match excessive spending by nonparticipating candidates. (Currently, a participating candidate is not provided with any additional public funds to match the spending of a nonparticipating candidate.)
- Providing the parties with some public financing to carry on the campaign during the interregnum period late in the primary season to the beginning of the general election season, when each candidate is again awarded public funds.

Section 527 political organizations have long been a bane in federal election law. These groups self-declare that their primary purpose is to affect elections under the tax code, but then claim that their activity should not be viewed as "federal election activity" subject to FECA and McCain-Feingold. Section 527 organizations have refused to abide by the same rules of contribution limits and source prohibitions that apply to the rest of us under federal campaign finance laws.

Prior to the soft money ban and electioneering communications requirement of McCain-Feingold, Section 527 groups were more of a nuisance in federal elections rather than emblematic of a breakdown in federal campaign finance law. The new, strengthened ban on soft money in federal elections under McCain-Feingold, however, has transformed these outside groups into a veritable "crack in the dam" of illegal money flowing into federal elections. In a single election cycle, Section 527 groups have expanded their soft money spending by 150 percent, and they promise to continue expanding their unique soft-money loophole in future elections.

Make no mistake about it: the Section 527 soft-money loophole does not favor the progressive community. These groups are now big-money conduits, and big money usually comes from special interests. Certainly, a few wealthy individuals pumped millions of dollars into Democratic-leaning Section 527 groups early in the 2004 elections. But they were soon outgunned by their Republican counterparts, who were instrumental in securing a second term for George Bush.

The Section 527 soft-money loophole, if left unchecked, will abruptly bring an end to reasonable limits on special-interest money in federal elections. Regardless of party affiliation, the end to limits on money in politics means that special interests will once again capture our candidates and our parties. Democrats in the soft-money world were every bit as smitten by big money and beholden to wealthy special interests as the Republicans. It took McCain-Feingold's ban on soft money to the parties to finally prompt the national Democratic Party to reach out to small contributors, expanding its donor base by several million small contributors and raising more funds through the Internet and direct mail in 2004 in hard money alone than it had raised in hard and soft money combined in any previous election cycle.[22]

It did not take long for MoveOn.org—one of the early Democratic-leaning Section 527 groups—to grasp this concept. Though the organization started up with a few large soft-money contributions, it soon realized that the bulk of its ongoing funds were coming in over the Internet in small, hard-money contributions from individuals. MoveOn.org realized that it could function more effectively as a regular political action committee, registered with the FEC, and chose to live, and flourish, under the contribution limits and source prohibitions of federal campaign finance laws.

The MoveOn.org experience should be the model for groups affiliated with progressive causes and sympathetic to progressive candidates. Reform politics is progressive politics. Progressives are being true to their core values when they advocate taking big money out of politics and reducing the role of special interests in government—and being true to your core values is essential if a political party is to thrive. Removing the Section 527 loophole is good politics for progressives and good policy for everyone. Progressives should make closing the last major soft-money loophole in federal elections a centerpiece of their reform agenda.

NOTES

1. *Buckley v. Valeo*, 424 U.S. 1 (1976).

2. The electioneering activities of Section 527 groups remained immune from effective disclosure until as recently as passage of the 2002 Brady-Lieberman Section 527 disclosure law. See Pub. L. No. 107-276 (2002) (codified in 26 U.S.C. §527 (2004)).

3. See, for example, David B. Magleby, ed., *Election Advocacy: Soft Money and Issue Advocacy in the 2000 Congressional Elections* (Salt Lake City: Center for the Study of Elections and Democracy, Brigham Young University, 2000), available at http://csed.byu.edu/Publications/Election%20Advocacy.html; and Craig Holman, "The End of Limits on Money in Politics: Soft Money Now Comprises the Largest Share of Party Spending on Television Ads in Federal Elections," Brennan Center for Justice, 2002, available at http://www .brennancenter.org/programs/downloads/mccain_feingold_softmoney0301.pdf.

4. Corporations were first prohibited from making campaign contributions in federal elections under the Tillman Act of 1907. The ban on corporate contributions was extended to labor unions under the 1943 War Labor Disputes Act (Smith-Connolly Act), which was renewed permanently in 1947 as the Taft-Hartley Act.

5. The Federal Election Campaign Act, as originally adopted in 1971, primarily comprised a campaign finance disclosure law. Following the Watergate scandals, FECA was amended in 1974 to include contribution limits as well as expenditure ceilings. The expenditure ceilings were later ruled unconstitutional as a violation of freedom of speech by the U.S. Supreme Court in its 1976 landmark decision, *Buckley v. Valeo*, but the contribution limits were held constitutional as part of a compelling state interest to address corruption or the appearance of corruption.

6. 11 C.F.R. §106.5(b) (2004).

7. The extent of the abuse of the soft money loophole in television advertising is well documented in Jonathan Krasno and Daniel Seltz, *Buying Time* (New York: Brennan Center for Justice, 2001); and Craig Holman and Luke McLoughlin, *Buying Time 2000* (New York: Brennan Center for Justice, 2002).

8. As part of a congressional compromise to secure passage of McCain-Feingold, the Levin Amendment was added to the law, allowing for a limited soft-money exception for voter registration activities of state and local party committees. Each state and local party committee may receive up to $10,000 in soft money per source, if permissible under state law. Money raised under this exception may not be used for federal candidate-specific or generic advertising, and the funds cannot be transferred between party committees.

9. David B. Magleby, ed., *Financing the 2000 Election* (Washington, D.C.: Brookings Institution Press, 2002), 144.

10. 2 U.S.C. §441(b).

11. *McConnell v. FEC*, 540 U.S. 93 (2003). The court invalidated only two modest provisions of McCain-Feingold: the ban on minors making campaign contributions, and a requirement that parties choose between either making independent expenditures or coordinated expenditures on behalf of federal candidates.

12. *McConnell v. FEC*, 660.

13. The court noted: "The notion that the First Amendment erects a rigid barrier between express and issue advocacy also cannot be squared with this Court's longstanding recognition that the presence or absence of magic words cannot meaningfully distinguish electioneering speech from a true issue ad. *Buckley*'s express advocacy line has not aided the legislative effort to combat real or apparent corruption, and Congress enacted BCRA to correct the flaws it found. Finally, because the components of [the] new definition of 'electioneering communication' are both easily understood and objectively determinable, the vagueness objection that persuaded the *Buckley* Court to limit FECA's reach to express advocacy is inapposite here" (*McConnell v. FEC*, 523).

14. In the 2005 congressional session, the pending Section 527 legislation included S. 271 in the Senate sponsored by Senators Trent Lott (R-Miss.), John McCain (R-Ariz.), and Russ Feingold (D-Wis.); and H.R. 513 in the House sponsored by Representatives Christopher Shays (R-Conn.) and Martin Meehan (D-Mass.).

15. Molly Ivins, "'Republicans for Clean Air': Pollution Fighters? Not Exactly," *San Jose Mercury News*, March 6, 2000.

16. "The Party Is Over, but All the Revelers Won't Go Home," *Public Citizen*, March 28, 2003.

17. Steve Weissman and Ruth Hassan, "BCRA and the 527 Groups," Campaign Finance Institute, draft chapter revised March 8, 2005, available at http://www.cfinst.org/studies/ElectionAfterReform/pdf/EAR_527Chapter.pdf, from *The Election after Reform: Money, Politics and the Bipartisan Campaign Reform Act*, ed. Michael J. Malbin (Lanham, Md.: Rowman & Littlefield, forthcoming).

18. David B. Magleby, J. Quin Monson, and Kelly D. Patterson, eds., *Dancing without Partners: How Candidates, Parties and Interest Groups Interact in the New Campaign Finance Environment* (Salt Lake City: Center for the Study of Elections and Democracy, Brigham Young University, 2005), available at http://csed.byu.edu/Index/DancingwithoutPartners.pdf.

19. David Holman, "Congress Shadows Free Speech," *American Spectator*, April 7, 2005.

20. Holman, "Congress Shadows Free Speech," 34.

21. Holman, "Congress Shadows Free Speech," 35.

22. The National Democratic Party raised $408 million in the 2002 election cycle in combined hard and soft money; in 2004, after McCain-Feingold, the Democratic Party raised $586 million in hard money alone. The National Republican Party raised $620 million in hard and soft money combined in the 2002 election cycle; in 2004, it raised $657 million in hard money alone (Federal Election Commission press releases, March 20, 2003, and February 18, 2005).

8

COMMUNICATING A PROGRESSIVE PHILOSOPHY

George Lakoff

To approach what unites progressives, we must first ask what divides them. Here are some of the common parameters that divide progressives from one another:

- Local interests
- Idealism versus pragmatism
- Radical change versus moderate change
- Militant versus moderate advocacy
- Types of thought processes: socioeconomic, identity politics, environmentalist, civil libertarian, spiritual, and antiauthoritarian[1]

Programs are a major problem for attempts at unity. As soon as a program is made specific, the differences must be addressed. Progressives tend to talk about programs. But programs are not what most Americans want to know about. Most Americans want to know what you stand for, whether your values are their values, what your principles are, what direction you want to take the country in. In public discourse, values trump programs, principles trump programs, policy directions trump programs. I believe that values, principles, and policy directions are exactly the things that can unite progressives, if they are crafted properly.

The reason that they can unite us is that they stand conceptually above all the things that divide us.

What follows is a detailed explication of each of those unifying ideas:

- First, values coming out of a basic progressive vision
- Second, principles that realize progressive values
- Third, policy directions that fit the values and principles
- And fourth, a brief ten-word philosophy that encapsulates all the above

THE BASIC PROGRESSIVE VISION

The basic progressive vision is of community—of America as family, a caring, responsible family. We envision an America where people care about each other, not just themselves, and act responsibly with strength and effectiveness for each other.

We are all in the same boat. Red states and blue states, progressives and conservatives, Republicans and Democrats. United, as we were for a brief moment just after September 11, not divided by a despicable culture war.

The Logic of Progressive Values

The progressive core values are family values—those of the responsible, caring family.

Caring and responsibility, carried out with strength. These core values imply the full range of progressive values. Here are those progressive values, together with the logic that links them to the core values.

Protection, fulfillment in life, fairness. When you care about someone, you want them to be protected from harm, you want their dreams to come true, and you want them to be treated fairly.

Freedom, opportunity, prosperity. There is no fulfillment without freedom, no freedom without opportunity, and no opportunity without prosperity.

Community, service, cooperation. Children are shaped by their communities. Responsibility requires serving and helping to shape your community. That requires cooperation.

Trust, honesty, open communication. There is no cooperation without trust, no trust without honesty, and no cooperation without open communication.

Just as these values follow from caring and responsibility, so every other progressive value follows from these. Equality follows from fairness, empathy is part of caring, diversity is from empathy and equality. Progressives not only share these values, but also share political principles that arise from these values.

Progressive Principles

Equity. What citizens and the nation owe each other. If you work hard; play by the rules; and serve your family, community, and nation, then the nation should provide a decent standard of living, as well as freedom, security, and opportunity.

Equality. Do everything possible to guarantee political equality and avoid imbalances of political power.

Democracy. Maximize citizen participation; minimize concentrations of political, corporate, and media power. Maximize journalistic standards. Establish publicly financed elections. Invest in public education. Bring corporations under stakeholder control, not just stockholder control.

Government for a better future. Government does what America's future requires and what the private sector cannot do—or is not doing—effectively, ethically, or at all. It is the job of government to promote and, if possible, provide sufficient protection, greater democracy, more freedom, a better environment, broader prosperity, better health, greater fulfillment in life, less violence, and the building and maintaining of public infrastructure.

Ethical business. Our values apply to business. In the course of making money by providing products and services, businesses should not adversely affect the public good, as defined by the above values.

Values-based foreign policy. The same values governing domestic policy should apply to foreign policy whenever possible.

Here are a few examples where progressive domestic policy translates into foreign policy:

- Protection translates into an effective military for defense and peacekeeping.
- Building and maintaining a strong community translates into building and maintaining strong alliances and engaging in effective diplomacy.
- Caring and responsibility translate into caring about and acting responsibly for the world's people; world health, hunger, poverty, and ecology; population control (and the best method, women's education); and rights for women, children, prisoners, refugees, and ethnic minorities.

All of these would be concerns of a values-based foreign policy.

POLICY DIRECTIONS

Given progressive values and principles, progressives can agree on basic policy directions. Policy directions are at a higher level than specific policies. Progressives divide on specific policy details while agreeing on directions. Here are some of the many policy directions they agree on.

The economy. An economy centered on innovation that creates millions of good-paying jobs and provides every American a fair opportunity to prosper.

Security. Through military strength, strong diplomatic alliances, and wise foreign and domestic policy, every American will be safeguarded at home, and America's role in the world will be strengthened by helping people around the world live better lives.

Health. Every American should have access to a state-of-the-art, affordable health care system.

Education. A vibrant, well-funded, and expanding public education system, with the highest standards for every child and school, where teachers nurture children's minds and often the children themselves, and where children are taught the truth about their nation—its wonders and its blemishes.

Early childhood. Every child's brain is shaped crucially by early experiences. We support high-quality early childhood education.

Environment. A clean, healthy, and safe environment for ourselves and our children: water you can drink and air you can breathe. Polluters pay for the damage they cause.

Nature. The natural wonders of our country are to be preserved for future generations.

Energy. We need to make a major investment in renewable energy, for the sake of millions of jobs that pay well, independence from Middle Eastern oil, improvements in public health, preservation of our environment, and the effort to halt global warming.

Openness. An open, efficient, and fair government that tells the truth to our citizens and earns the trust of every American.

Equal rights. We support equal rights in every area involving race, ethnicity, gender, and sexual orientation.

Protections. We support keeping and extending protections for consumers, workers, retirees, and investors.

These and many other policy directions follow from our values and our principles.

TEN-WORD PHILOSOPHIES

The conservatives have figured out their own values, principles, and directions, and have gotten them out in the public mind so effectively over the past thirty years that they can evoke them all in a ten-word philosophy: Strong Defense, Free Markets, Lower Taxes, Smaller Government,

Family Values. We progressives have a different ten-word philosophy, but it won't be as meaningful yet because it will take us a while to get our values, principles, and directions out there. My nomination for our ten-word philosophy versus theirs is the following:

Progressives:

- Stronger America
- Broad Prosperity
- Better Future
- Effective Government
- Mutual Responsibility

Conservatives:

- Strong Defense
- Free Markets
- Lower Taxes
- Smaller Government
- Family Values

A **stronger America** is not just about defense, but about every dimension of strength: our effectiveness in the world, our economy, our educational system, our health care system, our families, our communities, our environment, and so forth.

Broad prosperity is the effect that markets are supposed to bring about. But all markets are constructed for someone's benefit; no markets are completely free. Markets should be constructed for the broadest possible prosperity, and they haven't been.

Americans want and deserve a **better future**—economically, educationally, environmentally, and in all other areas of life—for themselves and their children. Lowering taxes, primarily for the super-rich elite, has had the effect of defunding programs that would make a better future possible in all these areas. The proper goal is a better future for all Americans.

Smaller government is, in conservative propaganda, supposed to eliminate waste. It is really about eliminating social programs. **Effective**

government is what we need our government to accomplish to create a better future.

Conservative family values are those of a strict father family— authoritarian, hierarchical, every man for himself, based around discipline and punishment. Progressives live by the best values of both families and communities: **mutual responsibility**, which is authoritative, equal, two-way, and based around caring, responsibility (both individual and social), and strength.

The remarkable thing is just how much progressives do agree on. These are just the things that voters tend to care about most: our values, our principles, and the direction in which we want to take the nation.

I believe that progressive values are traditional American values, that progressive principles are fundamental American principles, and that progressive policy directions point the way to where most Americans really want our country to go. The job of unifying progressives is really the job of bringing our country together around its finest traditional values.

NOTE

1. See George Lakoff, *Moral Politics: How Liberals and Conservatives Think* (Chicago: University of Chicago Press, 2002).

9

TEACHING PROGRESSIVES
TO "SPEAK AMERICAN"

David Kusnet

In accepting the Democratic nomination in 1992, Bill Clinton invoked a set of values—opportunity, responsibility, and community—that became the watchwords of his successful presidential campaign. His words evoked the value-laden 1980 acceptance speech delivered by Ronald Reagan, who called for "a new consensus with all those across the land who share a community of values embodied in these words: family, work, neighborhood, peace, and freedom."

Reagan and Clinton were speaking the language of normal life, evoking widely held moral values. They were elected and reelected against opponents who tended to speak the language of government and public policy. Each time, "speaking American" beat "speaking Bureaucratese." This plain lesson has been lost on progressives in recent years. Remember Arnold Schwarzenegger versus Gray Davis? George W. Bush versus Al Gore? Bush versus John Kerry? The conservative candidates sounded more like the regular people their policies injure or ignore.

So how can progressives present our causes and candidates in ways that make sense to most Americans, especially the great majority whose living standards have been flat-lining under George W. Bush? For someone who worked in union organizing and, later, in presidential campaigns during the 1980s and 1990s, the question has echoes of what Yogi

Berra called "déjà vu all over again." After all, we had just lost a presidential election to an aristocrat named George Bush, whose economic program boiled down to tax breaks for multimillionaires but who managed to convince a narrow majority of the voters that his opponent was some sort of cultural elitist. And our candidate, a high-minded fellow from Massachusetts, seemed unable to respond effectively to those attacks or to connect emotionally with most voters.

Yes, that's the story of the 2004 presidential campaign. But it's the story of 1988 as well. And, if progressives could find a way to rebound from losing to the first President Bush, then we can do it again. I know because I saw us do it.

THE 1988 POPULIST REVIVAL

Back in September 1988, when his presidential candidacy was taking a pounding from Republicans calling him a "Harvard Yard elitist," a "card-carrying member of the ACLU," and a "Massachusetts liberal" who didn't like school prayer and the Pledge of Allegiance, Michael Dukakis took me aside at a debate preparation meeting and told me to stop putting attacks on "country-club Republicans" in my drafts for his speeches. He didn't like "attacking straw-men" and "that divisive stuff," he explained. "It isn't me."

Dukakis's dignity was admirable, but by October 15 he was down to 38 percent of the national vote, heading for a landslide loss on the scale of George McGovern in 1972. So he and his high command decided to give "that divisive stuff" a try.

I had a hand in writing a new stump speech that explained why Dukakis would be good for the great majority of Americans, while the elder George Bush would benefit the privileged and powerful. The speech drew a compelling contrast between Democratic policies that would help most people and Republican policies that would help the fortunate few. At rallies around the country, a fired-up Dukakis would take off his jacket, loosen his tie, and tell his audiences, "I'm on your side":

> George Bush [senior] is for the people on Easy Street. I'm for the people
> on Main Street. . . . George Bush is for the people who already have it

made. I want to help every family make it. . . . George Bush wants a tax break for the wealthiest one percent of all Americans. I want to help your kids have the chance to go to college.

When he was finished speaking, loudspeakers would blare "Fortunate Son" by Credence Clearwater Revival: "Some folks are born silver spoon in hand. . . . It ain't me, it ain't me, I ain't no millionaire's son." Hard as it may be to imagine, the crowds would cheer. In just two weeks, a revitalized Dukakis climbed eight points in the polls, recalling the last-minute surges of the aggressively populist Truman and Humphrey campaigns. It was not enough to win but it allowed Dukakis to avoid humiliation and protect Democrats running for other offices. Progressives began to wonder: What if our candidates, causes, and organizations thought, talked, and—most important of all—acted that way year in and year out, not only in the last two weeks of losing presidential campaigns?

SPEAKING AMERICAN: ROUND ONE

After the 1988 election brought progressives their fifth defeat in six presidential cycles, there was so much rethinking going on in the liberal community that journalist Sidney Blumenthal called those discussions "The Conversation." My contribution was a short paperback called *Speaking American*. It tried to explain how progressive candidates and movements could do what even the mild-mannered, buttoned-down, too-decent-for-his-own-good Dukakis did in those last weeks of his losing campaign: connect with working Americans by addressing their economic anxieties and their sense that the system was stacked against them.

Looking back on the battles we'd lost in the 1980s, it was impossible to avoid the conclusion that progressives needed to do more than be populist about economics, important as that is. We also had to establish that we had the same basic moral values—and the willingness to put them into practice—as hardworking people who were threatened by street crime, drug trafficking, a popular culture that glorified destructive behavior, and a welfare system that (at that time) seemed to subsidize not working or forming a family.

Lee Atwater, the elder Bush's political advisor, said after the 1988 election that liberals win when economic populism is on people's minds and conservatives win when cultural populism is on their minds. How can progressives establish that we share the same basic moral standards as our fellow citizens—and that we're tough enough to defend decent people against street criminals or rogue states—so that people will pay attention when we talk about jobs, wages, health care, and economic opportunity? And how can we say all those things in ways that make sense to most Americans, address their concerns, appeal to their values, and inspire them to take action? In other words, how can we "speak American"?

One copy of my paperback found its way to Bill Clinton. He didn't need any lessons about speaking plainly and persuasively, but, early in 1992, he did need a campaign staff. When he hired me, he quoted and corrected several passages from the book, explaining that he wanted to be a "pro-growth" populist who would explain why improving educational opportunities, providing more job training, and making sure that everyone has health insurance would all make the economy more successful.

For the next eight years, Clinton proved he could speak American as well as any public figure of our time, winning election and reelection, surviving impeachment, and doing many things progressives wanted (raising the minimum wage, increasing tax credits for the working poor, and presiding over a full-employment economy) as well as some things we didn't (passing NAFTA with little in the way of labor standards).

Clinton also did his best to teach progressives to speak American the way he did in 1992. Understanding that most Americans, including the working poor, either consider themselves or aspire to be "middle class," he pitched his candidacy to "the forgotten middle class" who "work hard and play by the rules." He convinced the most volatile voters—white working-class families—to listen to him because he said things they didn't expect national Democrats to say any more, declaring "governments don't raise children, families do" and promising to "end welfare as we know it." Having established that he wasn't part of the cultural elite, he turned his fire toward irresponsible economic elites, attacking the "rip-off artists who looted the S&Ls" and corporate CEOs who "sell their companies and their workers and their country down the river."

These populist zingers weren't just applause lines; they reflected a new and coherent political outlook that appealed to Americans' most basic beliefs. Clinton wasn't attacking CEOs just because they were rich, and he certainly wasn't attacking the welfare system because it tried to help the poor. Instead, he was suggesting that every American should behave responsibly and that we should expect the most from those who have received the most—the people at the top of the economic and political ladders.

While political reporters and his own speechwriters may have tired of the rhetorical triad that defined Clinton's philosophy—"opportunity, responsibility, and community"—it addressed a middle-class populism that differed from the dominant currents in both conservatism and liberalism. Unlike the corporate conservatives who dominated the Republican Party, Clinton recognized that America owes all people opportunities for education and employment. Fundamentally, he was willing to declare that America must be a community—and he made clear that community includes everyone, saying, "We're all in this together, we're all going up or down together, and we don't have a person to waste." In a departure from post-1960s cultural liberalism, he also insisted that every American should be expected to behave responsibly and that expanded opportunities should come with expanded obligations, as exemplified by his proposal to link college assistance to national service.

This rhetoric served Clinton well, protecting him against the sort of cultural populist potshots that were so damaging to Dukakis and later to Al Gore and John Kerry. It also provided the best rationale for progressive public policies by contending that we need to regulate corporate behavior because, from the savings and loan scandal two decades ago to the Enron scandal more recently, CEOs can use their enormous economic power irresponsibly. And we should reward responsible behavior by working Americans by cutting taxes for the working poor, raising the minimum wage, and restoring the right to organize unions.

LEARNING FROM GEORGE W. BUSH

So, if Clinton got it right, why has so much gone wrong since the Supreme Court awarded the 2000 election to the younger George Bush?

Fast-forward a few years. Yes, the September 11, 2001, terror attacks made national security more important than it had been since the end of the Cold War. Yes, the cultural divides that Clinton straddled have hardened once again. And in his own way, George W. Bush speaks American, too. He uses everyday words, short sentences, simple statements of right and wrong that suggest he is decent and decisive, and references to Biblical passages, prayers, and hymns that are embedded in his text, rather than explicitly quoted, thus appealing to the faithful without antagonizing secular voters.

At the same time, national Democrats have been tongue-tied. They have failed to do what Bill Clinton did so well: speak in ways that fire up their base while winning swing voters. Sixteen years after Dukakis floundered through most of his campaign without rousing populist passions or reassuring voters about his reliability on social issues and national security, another nominee from Massachusetts, John Kerry, also failed to make a compelling case on economics and to present himself as culturally mainstream. Somehow, this fiscally conservative senator with a patrician background was persuaded that he must not sound "too populist" on economics, with the result that he dropped one of his few applause lines, an attack on "Benedict Arnold CEOs" who were sending American jobs overseas. Instead, he ended up offering detailed programs for the economy, education, and health care without presenting them in ways that most voters remembered. Although he frequently quoted the Bible and successfully identified himself with the police officers and firefighters who protect the people, he said little that was memorable, much less stereotype-shattering, about social and cultural issues. Thus, Kerry actually ran far behind Bush among working-class whites—the very voters who used to be the Democrats' strongest supporters.

SPEAKING AMERICAN: ROUND TWO

Speaking clearly and compellingly to the entire electorate, especially working Americans, isn't all it takes for progressives to prevail. But we can't win without persuading people. So how can progressives speak American again?

Lead with Principles, Not Programs

Progressives tend to be part of what a Bush administration official famously called "the reality-based community." We believe in the power of facts to persuade and the potential of government to do good. This can lead us to talk interminably about the dimensions of social problems we oppose and the details of the social programs we propose. Not surprisingly, many people doze off while we drone on.

Rather than lead with data and details, we should begin by saying what we believe—because our beliefs explain why we think things are wrong and need to be put right. For instance, an argument for raising the minimum wage might begin like this: "People who work full-time should not have to raise their kids in poverty." Then, it would explain the problem—millions of kids have parents who work for poverty wages—and set forth the solution: raising wages to a level that a family can live on.

Be Tough and Caring

Leading with principles sounds like the lesson many progressives have drawn from linguistics guru George Lakoff, who wisely advises that progressives need to set the terms of debate (he calls it "framing") and not use the other side's catchwords (as when conservatives call taxes on huge inheritances the "death tax"). In this book, he too makes the case that progressives should lead with principles, not programs.

But it is important not to misunderstand his observation that the progressive–conservative divide reflects two views of parenting—toughness or nurturing—and conclude that progressives should frame issues in ways that make people think like nurturing parents. Lakoff says the core progressive values of caring and responsibility should be carried out with strength. Most people understand the need for both approaches— for being tough and caring—and want their leaders and the policies they pursue to reflect both sets of virtues.

Especially in the post-9/11 era, voters want leaders who are ready and able to defend America. Similarly, voters favor public policies that combine toughness and caring—setting standards while fully funding public schools, helping public aid recipients find jobs while raising the minimum wage and making sure their jobs come with health insurance and the right to organize unions.

For those with long memories, Robert F. Kennedy exemplified the style of leadership that set high standards for every segment of society, especially the most privileged. In the United Kingdom, Prime Minister Tony Blair spoke volumes about his own tough-and-nurturing approach with his slogan, "Tough on crime, tough on the causes of crime." Here in the United States, as Bill Clinton has suggested, progressives should claim credit for some of the "tough" things he did—reforming welfare, balancing the federal budget, and putting more police on the street— and then move on to address social problems such as the plight of those without health insurance.

If I sound like I'm revisiting old arguments, well, I admit I am. As far back as 1984, when I worked as a speechwriter for Walter Mondale, I was frustrated by the campaign's failure to stress the fact that both Mondale and his running mate, Geraldine Ferraro, were former prose-cutors. In 1988, I was even more exasperated that Dukakis delivered only one major speech about crime. In *Speaking American*, I entitled one section "Tough and Caring," making a point that many progressives still fail to grasp: toughness is intrinsic to populism. After all, working-class voters experience the harsh side of life, and they want leaders who are tough on crime, drugs, and social breakdown—and also tough on corporate wrongdoers and exploitative employers. Try this thought ex-periment: You're running for president of a local union. Do you want to present yourself only as nurturing—or as tough and nurturing?

Use the Power of Populism

While progressives need to cut our losses on social issues like crime, we win on economic issues—building prosperity that benefits everyone who's willing to work hard. Far from blurring distinctions with Republi-cans on economic issues, progressives should present themselves as fighting for regular people against economic elites and explain why the best way to expand the economy is to invest in working people's skills and make sure that they share in the gains they achieve by working harder and smarter.

Yes, that means looking out for the very debates and distinctions that conservatives characterize as "class warfare." For instance, John Edwards has developed a persuasive way of distinguishing between the conservatives' treatment of taxes on "work" (the federal income and payroll taxes, and state and local sales and property taxes) and taxes on "wealth" (taxes on corporate dividends and large inheritances). On the other hand, most progressives failed to develop the distinction between how the Bush administration made it more difficult for everyday families to file for bankruptcy while making it easier for corporations to use bankruptcy as an excuse to default on pension obligations to their retirees.

Speak in Parables

Effective oratory relies on fables as well as frames, and progressives should make use of four populist parables that are part of American culture:

1. *Rot at the Top.* The classic populist parable holds that those with the most power and privilege—Washington muck-a-mucks, multimillionaire CEOs, and others with wealth and influence—have betrayed the larger community. Corporate wrongdoing at Enron and WorldCom—and practices that are legal but harmful, such as moving operations offshore to escape taxes in this country—call to mind "rot at the top," a phrase that former Labor Secretary Robert Reich popularized during the 1980s. So does self-serving or misleading behavior by government officials or leaders from any other sector of society.

2. *Virtue Unrewarded.* The flip-side of unpunished wrongdoing by the big shots is unrewarded responsibility by regular people. When Bill Clinton talked about how "people who worked hard and played by the rules" were being overlooked, he appealed to the widely held belief that people who do honest work, pay their taxes, live within the law, and do right by their community are not getting the respect and rewards that they have earned. That's why the working poor, the middle-class taxpayer, and the responsible businessperson all are sympathetic figures. And that's why slogans like

"make work pay" generate wide support for living-wage ordinances, union organizing drives, and programs such as child care that help people move from welfare to employment.

3. *The Caring Community.* Americans believe in helping each other out and sharing life's benefits and burdens. For all our individualism, most of us don't believe that people make it entirely on their own; we know we need a community behind us. In difficult times, such as the post-9/11 world, Americans want everyone to contribute, especially those with the most advantages. Progressives can use rhetorical jujitsu against President Bush: If the nation really is besieged, then how can we justify new benefits for the wealthy and new burdens on the rest of us?

4. *The People Rising.* Our nation's primal parable is the American Revolution: the people rising, peaceably at first, to demand the right to govern themselves. From the tax rebellions of the 1970s and 1980s to the recall initiative that made Arnold Schwarzenegger governor of California, conservatives have presented themselves as modern-day Minutemen. But so did progressives during the 1960s and 1970s, particularly during the civil rights movement, the women's movement, and the peace movement. All these successful movements, whether of the Left, Right, or Center, have cast their causes as something larger than the redress of specific grievances. Instead, they have declared that the future of democracy rests with the success of their cause. Thus, these movements themselves became models of democracy, with tax rebels recalling the Boston Tea Party and the civil rights movement adopting the rhetoric of the Declaration of Independence.

Speak with Your Natural Voice

Rhetoric is not "one size fits all." Progressives need to avoid prepackaged pronouncements, lest we run the risk of sounding programmed— and not sounding like the individuals we are.

In different ways, John Edwards, John McCain, and Howard Dean get people to listen to them because they don't sound like other politicians. Edwards speaks like an authentic populist because he doesn't sound patronizing, down to the fine points of his phrasing. He talks about "regular people," not "ordinary" or "average" people. He doesn't say, "I'll fight for you"—he says, "I'm fighting for the people I grew up with." Details, yes, but they distinguish him from the last liberal politician you heard or from career politicians and stiff patricians who present themselves as champions of people very different from themselves. For his part, McCain actually answers the questions reporters pose to him, a refreshing departure from politicians who recite planned responses whether or not they bear any relationship to the questions that were asked. At his best, Dean presents himself as an everyday citizen who speaks the language of empowerment. During his unsuccessful campaign for the 2004 presidential nomination, he would tell supporters, "You have the power"—a much less patronizing appeal than "I will fight for you."

Whether it's being offered by a candidate or a cause, fresh phrasing makes people pay attention, which is the first step toward persuasion. Back in 1988, Jesse Jackson had a new and vivid way of talking about the working poor—he would say, "They take the early bus." Four years earlier, in his convention keynote, Mario Cuomo used the quintessential American metaphor of a wagon train that doesn't leave the children and the elderly behind to describe a society that cares about the most vulnerable. Twenty years later, in his keynote speech to the 2004 Democratic convention, Barack Obama got a national audience to listen to him by talking like a human being, saying his parents shared "an unlikely love," that as a youngster he was "a skinny kid with a funny name," and that a soldier he spoke to was "a good-looking kid with an easy smile."

Following the 2004 election, during which Bush benefited from the support of religious conservatives, many progressives are seasoning their rhetoric with Biblical quotations and invocations of moral values. But these statements only make sense when they are rooted in the subject that's being discussed and the person who's doing the talking. For public figures who are comfortable testifying to their faith—for instance, Jesse Jackson, Jimmy Carter, or Joe Lieberman—it is completely natural to quote scripture and lead with moral precepts. As with George W. Bush, their personal philosophies are so influenced by religion and their public rhetoric is so infused with scriptural references that any other way of talking would sound lifeless.

But for public figures who aren't religious or those whose traditions don't stress public witnessing, it sounds stilted or worse to work a few Bible quotations into every public appearance or to begin an Earth Day speech by saying that the Bible calls upon us to be stewards of our natural environment.

It is far better for secular progressives to emulate Hillary Rodham Clinton, who has given morally serious speeches about such social issues as making popular culture more family friendly or reducing abortions while protecting women's right to choose. Just as Bill Clinton spoke of making abortion "safe, legal, and rare," she has addressed the moral concerns of social conservatives and many other Americans as well without abandoning her commitments to free expression and an inclusive America. In other examples of how public discourse can be infused with moral concerns, Franklin D. Roosevelt and John F. Kennedy used the language of justice and mercy to address the great public issues of their times—economic justice in the 1930s and civil rights in the 1960s. As it happens Hillary Clinton is religious, as was FDR, while JFK had to answer accusations that his Catholic faith would have too much influence over his presidency. But for each of them, their oratory exemplifies how public argument can reflect mainstream moral values, not the dogma of one denomination.

ENGAGING ORDINARY VOTERS

Appealing to common values, developing populist parables, and speaking engaging, everyday language—that is how progressives can communicate to our fellow citizens and persuade all Americans to follow their best instincts and their best interests.

Is "speaking American" sufficient to bring about social change? Of course not. But it is essential. As George Orwell wrote, our ways of writing and speaking reflect our ways of thinking and acting. If we can't explain something in plain English and if we can't justify it in terms of basic moral values, then maybe we should think twice before advocating it at all.

10

FIRE THE CONSULTANTS!

Amy Sullivan

If you were a Democrat running as a first-time candidate for the U.S. Senate in 2002, Joe Hansen was most likely a familiar part of your life. As the field director for the Democratic Senatorial Campaign Committee (DSCC), Hansen was responsible for recruiting promising candidates, and then for getting the nascent campaigns off to a running start. In the first overwhelming days of your campaign, Joe was a lifeline. He took you out to dinner for pep talks, broke down the fundraising process into something almost manageable, walked you through the selection of campaign staff and consultants, and promised that—if you proved you were a serious candidate by putting together the right team—the DSCC would happily write the checks that might make the difference when things really heated up in the fall. And when it came to choosing just the right firm to design and produce the fliers, postcards, and door hangers that would blanket your state in the closing weeks of the campaign, Joe recommended the very best consultant he knew: Joe Hansen.

In addition to his job at the DSCC, Hansen was also a partner in the direct mail firm of Ambrosino, Muir & Hansen. His sales pitch must have been effective—Democrats in nine of the closest Senate contests in 2002 signed up with Hansen, including Jeanne Shaheen in New

Hampshire, Max Cleland in Georgia, and Alex Sanders in South Carolina. The day after the election, only two (Tim Johnson in South Dakota and Mark Pryor in Arkansas) were still standing.

Despite widespread grumbling about his aggressive tactics, Hansen was still part of the DSCC as of early 2005 (he stepped down as field director midway through 2002 as criticism mounted; officially, he now operates as a consultant for the committee). What's most surprising, though, is that Democratic candidates continue to hire him despite his losing record. After his candidates lost seven of nine close races in 2002, Hansen was again a man in demand during the 2004 election cycle. His firm handled five of the most competitive Senate races in that year, including the two—Tony Knowles in Alaska and Erskine Bowles in North Carolina—that prognosticators thought were most winnable. Only one of Hansen's candidates, Ken Salazar in Colorado, pulled out a victory.

Hansen is part of a clique of Washington consultants who, through their insider ties, continue to get rewarded with business even after losing continually. Pollster Mark Mellman is popular among Democrats because he tells them what they so desperately want to hear: Their policies are sound, Americans really agree with them more than with Republicans, and if they just repeat their mantras loud enough, voters will eventually embrace the party. As Noam Scheiber pointed out in a *New Republic* article following the great Democratic debacle of '02, Mellman was, perhaps more than anyone else, the architect of that defeat.[1] As the DSCC's recommended pollster, he advised congressional Democrats to ignore national security and Iraq in favor of an endless campaign about prescription drugs and education. After the party got its clock cleaned based on his advice, Mellman probably should have been exiled but was instead . . . promoted. He became the lead pollster for John Kerry's presidential campaign, where he proffered eerily similar advice—stress domestic policy, stay away from attacking Bush—to much the same effect.

Hansen and Mellman are joined by the poster boy of Democratic social promotion, Bob Shrum. Over his 30-year career, Shrum has worked on the campaigns of seven losing presidential candidates—from George McGovern to Bob Kerrey—capping his record with a leading role in the disaster that was the Gore campaign. Yet, instead of abiding by the "seven strikes and you're out" rule, Democrats have continued to pay top dollar for his services. Although Shrum has never put anyone in the White House, in the bizarro world of Democratic politics, he's seen as a kingmaker—merely hiring the media strategist gives a candidate such instant credibility with big-ticket liberal funders that John Kerry and John Edwards fought a fierce battle heading into the 2004 primaries to lure Shrum to their camps. Ultimately, Shrum chose Kerry, and on Nov. 3, he extended his perfect losing record.

After their devastating loss in November of 2004, Democrats cast about for reasons why their party has come up short three election cycles in a row and have debated what to do. Should they lure better candidates? Talk more about morality? Adopt a harder line on national security? But one of the most obvious and least discussed reasons Democrats continue to lose is their consultants. Every sports fan knows that if a team boasts a losing record several seasons in a row, the coach has to be replaced with someone who can win. Yet when it comes to political consultants, Democrats seem incapable of taking this basic managerial step.

A major reason for that reluctance is that Democrats simply won't talk openly about the problem. Shrum did eventually take some heat publicly during the 2004 campaign when the contrast between his losing record and his high position in the troubled Kerry campaign became too stark to ignore.[2] But in general, a Mafia-like code of *omerta* operates. Few insiders dare complain about the hammerlock loser consultants have on the process—neither the professional campaign operatives whom the consultants hire nor the journalists to whom the consultants feed juicy inside-the-room detail. In the process of investigating the Democratic consulting world, I interviewed two dozen Democratic Party leaders, operatives, and others. Few had a good thing to say about the consultant oligarchy. Yet virtually no one would talk on the record. The exceptions were those who have gotten out of the business of working for political candidates, such as Dan Gerstein, a former advisor to Sen. Joe Lieberman (D-Conn.). "If a company like General Motors had the same image problem that the Democratic Party does, they would fire the guys responsible," Gerstein told me. But not Democrats. "We don't just hire those guys," Gerstein said, "we give them bonuses."

A NUMBER OF PAYCHECKS

Most big-name consultants' national careers begin with a breakthrough success. For Joe Hansen, that moment came in 1996, when he managed Tim Johnson's upset of incumbent senator Larry Pressler in South Dakota. The slightly chubby, sandy-haired operative had been involved with political races for a number of years by that time, but the Johnson campaign made his reputation as a premier field organizer and attracted the attention of Democratic Senate leader Tom Daschle, who hired Hansen to run his own reelection campaign two years later. Daschle was never in danger of losing (he eventually won by 26 percentage points), so Hansen had time to step in as campaign doctor for other races, saving the seats of both Sen. Patty Murray in Washington and Sen. Harry Reid in Nevada. With a gruff, take-no-guff manner—even those who consider him a friend say he can be explosive and overbearing—Hansen can whip a campaign into shape with his instinctive knack for field operations, and talent for moving around money, material, and manpower.

It's a skill that is sorely needed at the party campaign committees, where Democrats consistently grapple with the considerable spending advantage their Republican counterparts enjoy. After the 1998 cycle, Hansen assumed the role of DSCC executive director, a position he held for five months before clashes with the equally aggressive committee chair Sen. Robert Torricelli (D-N.J.) led him to step down and become DSCC field director instead.[3] In truth, the apparent demotion was a good move for Hansen, who is at his best in the field, not managing staff in a Washington suite.

And all might have been well if Hansen hadn't answered the siren call of the consulting world. It's not hard to understand why many political operatives become consultants—when you work for a campaign, you do a lot of work for one candidate and draw one salary; when you work as a consultant, you do similar work for several different candidates and collect several different paychecks. But you also dilute your focus and divide your loyalties. Moreover, individuals who excel in a specialized area like polling or fieldwork typically try to migrate to higher-paying, higher-prestige work as strategists and message maestros. Shrum is, by all accounts, an excellent wordsmith, but he has no genius for strategy and very little feel for what makes Middle America tick—he is, after all, best known for writing a concession speech for Ted Kennedy's failed presidential bid in 1980. Similarly, Chris Lehane and Mark Fabiani are two of the most effective opposition researchers and spinmeisters in the business. But they were probably out of their depth when they took charge of retired Gen. Wesley Clark's run for the presidency as his lead consultants.

Hansen is no exception—he is brilliant at executing campaign tactics in the field but as a consultant he is not playing to those strengths. Candidates who used Hansen as their direct mail consultant in 2002 found that he was less than adept at turning his field magic into effective campaign products. One of the fliers I saw for a 2004 Hansen client had a slapped-together look to it. Accompanying the text were photos of, presumably, area residents—upon closer inspection, one turned out to be Hansen himself.

How does Hansen defend his performance and any potential conflict between his roles as DSCC representative and private consultant? Not very aggressively. After I made numerous attempts over two weeks to get an interview with Hansen, he replied with a one-paragraph e-mail, in which he listed the three victorious senatorial and three winning gubernatorial races that his company had handled in 2004, and concluded, redundantly, "Our firm has an unmatched record of success that no other firm can match." The e-mail came from Hansen's DSCC account.

THE CONSULTANT'S HAT

It's important to understand that even for experienced politicians—mayors, governors, representatives—a Senate run can be an intimidating challenge. It involves courting an entirely new world of donors by proving to Washington fundraisers and party leaders that you are a serious contender. Jeremy Wright, who served as the political director for Oregon Senate candidate Bill Bradbury's race in the spring and early summer of 2002, says that candidates are almost required to run two parallel campaigns, "one to get voters to vote for you and the other to get D.C. money by putting together the right consultants to show you're for real." For Democratic candidates in the few targeted races every cycle that are actually competitive, winning without the financial support of the

DSCC (or its sister organization, the Democratic Congressional Campaign Committee) is nearly impossible. While the candidates are grateful for the infusion of cash in the form of committee-sponsored polling, fliers, and commercials, the money comes with strings.

Officially, no favoritism exists. "We don't push one consultant over another," a DSCC spokeswoman told me. "It's more of an informational thing, telling candidates about good people who do a lot of Senate races." But Democrats who have worked on targeted races describe a reality in which they are strongly encouraged—often with the reminder that precious funds hang in the balance—to select recommended consultants. "The campaign was pretty paranoid about making sure the DSCC was backing us," explains one veteran of an unsuccessful 2002 Senate race. "We needed the cash. So of course, we were going to go with the consultants they recommended."

As the first man-on-the-ground, Hansen's contact with budding campaigns was early and often. "That person has a very large advantage in being able to shape the team," one of Hansen's consulting competitors told me. "You bond with the candidate from the get-go at a pretty stressful time when they're deciding whether to run and how to do it."

The setup puts candidates—who are loath to alienate the campaign committee whose financial assistance they desperately need—in a tricky spot. Even when working with experienced consultants, candidates need to retain some ability to disagree with a proposed idea or strategy. That's hard enough when the consultant is recommended by the party committee. But when the consultant actually *is* the party committee, the candidate's discretion stays sealed in a tight box. "It was an interesting dynamic, I'll say that," Wright says. "When Joe signed us up, he was on staff for the DSCC. We'd work on DS[CC] stuff during the day, and then he'd take us out to dinner and put on his consultant hat."

THE LEVEL OF THEIR INCOMPETENCE

This Peter Principle effect of Democratic operatives rising—or muscling their way—up to the level of their incompetence, happens for a simple reason: The consultants are filling a vacuum. After all, someone has to formulate the message that a candidate can use to win the voters' support. Conservatives have spent 30 years and billions of dollars on think tanks and other organizations to develop a set of interlinked policies and language that individual Republican candidates and campaigns can adopt in plug-and-play fashion. Liberals are far behind in this message development game. Indeed, most Democratic elected officials have been running recently on warmed-up leftovers from the Clinton brain trust, ideas which were once innovative but are now far from fresh. With little else to go on, consultants—many of whom came to prominence during the Clinton years—have clung to old ideas and strategies like security blankets. "Democratic consultants are being asked to fill a role they're not suited to," says Simon Rosenberg, head of the New Democratic Network, "to come up with ideas and electoral strategy in addition to media strategy."

Rosenberg hints at a second Democratic deficit: The party has no truly brilliant strategists in positions of power. Such talent is always rare in both parties and tends to come out of the political hinterlands, often as part of a winning presidential campaign team. Jimmy Carter's 1976 campaign was waged by a crew of Georgia political operatives with the help of unconventional pollster Pat Caddell. Four years later, Reagan defeated Carter by relying on a California-based gang of professionals. James Carville and Paul Begala were largely unknown before they took Bill Clinton to the White House. And outside the South, the team of Karl Rove, Karen Hughes, and Mark McKinnon weren't much less obscure when they put together the strategy for George W. Bush's winning 2000 campaign.

It's no coincidence that the brightest and most effective consultants have come to prominence by working for governors. The nature of both governing from and campaigning for the statehouse requires a governor to lean on consultants who know local politics and concerns intimately. The adage that all politics is local often gets dismissed in Washington as too obvious to be worth repeating, but the successful state consultant takes it to heart, learning the priorities of voters and tailoring messages to meet those concerns instead of imposing a top-down, national agenda. As a result, governors who run for president are often surrounded by advisors who are trained to ferret out the issues voters really care about, instead of figuring out ways to make voters care about the candidate's issues. Senators, on the other hand, are already so engulfed in the Washington consultancy world that they turn first to the biggest and best names, who rarely turn out to have their fingers on the pulse of the average voter.

Republicans have proven much more adept than Democrats at giving their best talent a national stage. While Democrats have permitted a Washington consultancy class to become comfortably entrenched, it appears that Republicans have effectively begun to pension off their own establishment. "The D.C. consultants for the GOP have their list of clients, but they're definitely on the outside looking in," Chuck Todd, editor of *National Journal's Political Hotline*, told me. "The Bush people have been very careful to give them work . . . but they're not in the inner circle." In 2004, seasoned Washington media strategist Alex Castellanos worked just with a handful of safe congressional races and a few unsuccessful primary challengers. Meanwhile, nearly every tight Senate race (North Carolina, Alaska, Oklahoma, South Dakota, Florida) was handled by a Tampa-based firm, The Victory Group.

Republicans, of course, don't have any natural monopoly on strategic talent—they just give their best young strategists chances to run the biggest national races. In all likelihood, there is another Karl Rove or James Carville out in the Democratic hinterlands, who ought to be playing essential roles in the most important races. It might be David Axelrod in Chicago, who developed the media strategy for the then-unknown Sen. Barack Obama's (D-Ill.) primary campaign; West Coast strategists Paul Goodwin and Amy Simon, who helped Democrats regain the legislature in Washington state; or even unconventional D.C.-based consultants like Anna Bennett, the pollster who engineered Melissa Bean's upset of veteran Rep. Phil Crane (R-Ill.) in November 2004. But any new talent will likely remain on the national margins—running races for Congress and judgeships—until someone breaks up the consultant oligarchy.

TAKING CARE OF DEAD WEIGHT

The electoral system takes care of dead weight when it comes to politicians. The proof is in the political wreckage evident after yet another year of Democratic defeats at the polls. Dick Gephardt—after 10 years at the helm of the Democratic minority in the House—moved back home to Missouri after the 2004 elections. John Kerry returned to the Senate instead of stretching out his legs in the Oval Office. The consultants, however, move on to another campaign. After his firm pocketed a $5-million paycheck following the election,[4] Shrum vacationed in Tuscany and then moved on to his next gig, Sen. Jon Corzine's (D-N.J.) gubernatorial race. Mellman continues to line up clients. As for Hansen, his connection to Daschle might not help him now that the South Dakotan has vacated the Democratic leader's office. But he's still the consultant for current Senate Minority Leader Harry Reid.

There are glimmers of hope that Democrats are coming around to the fact that you get better results when you reward success and punish— or at least don't encourage—losing track records. *The Hill* newspaper, which tracks congressional politics, reported in February 2005 that both Reid and his House counterpart, Nancy Pelosi (D-Calif.) "plan to shake up the Democratic political consulting community and break the grip that a small number of consultants have had on strategy and contracts." They would do well to pass that order along to Sen. Chuck Schumer (D-N.Y.), who is directing the DSCC for the next election cycle, and Rahm Emanuel (D-Ill.), his counterpart at the DCCC, as both organizations continue to do business with the same cadre of unsuccessful consultants as in the past. But rank-and-file political aides are eager to see the power of these consultants diminish. Many cheered Shrum's announcement early in 2005 that he planned to decamp from Washington, D.C., scale back his consulting activities, and focus primarily on teaching at New York University. An early version of this chapter, published in the *Washington Monthly* in January 2005, generated near-universal glee from offices on Capitol Hill that have dealt first-hand with losing Democratic consultants. These emperors have no clothes. Fortunately for the Democratic Party, there are plenty of fully clothed consultants ready to step in and take their place.

NOTES

1. Noam Scheiber, "Exit Poll," *The New Republic*, February 24, 2003.

2. See, for example, http://www.cbsnews.com/stories/2004/09/14/politics/main 643438.shtml; http://www.washingtonpost.com/wp-dyn/articles/A9895-2004 Sep9.html; and http://www.commondreams.org/views04/0918-01.htm.

3. Rachel Van Dongen and John Bresnahan, "Torricelli Shakes Up DSCC Staff; Fox Will Replace Hansen as Executive Director," *Roll Call*, May 10, 1999.

4. Thomas B. Edsall and James V. Grimaldi, "How the Two Parties Split their Millions," *The Washington Post*, December 30, 2004.

POWERING UP
INTERNET CAMPAIGNS

Zephyr Teachout

Politics: the mess of it, the fight of it, the high stakes of electoral combat—these things are naturally compelling to people. The Constitution's framers counted on the innate appeal of politics to engage a nation and maintain a republic, and for most of our history we have responded to their call. It's in our nature. Human beings are political animals.

The current era of cynical, television-centered politics is an anomaly, characterized by would-be voters turned into casual viewers of a political process seemingly too distant or irrelevant to engage them. It's no wonder that people would roll their eyes at made-for-television presidential "town meetings" hailing from the antiseptic confines of a TV studio, and at interchangeable anchors puffing up their self-importance while magnifying the foibles of political leaders. But give people the means to participate—meaningfully—and they will provide the motivation.

The Internet's biggest contribution to this mix is that it enables collective action on an almost unimaginable scale. Flexible political communities (local and national) can easily form, and people who do engage can immediately experience the impacts of their actions. If the Democratic Party—or a wing of the Democratic Party, or an affiliated progressive organization outside the Democratic Party—can seize this moment in history and start seeing itself as a service organization, serving the needs of its constituents to engage in politics, then with the help of the Internet it can revolutionize political involvement.

Our task is to solve the collective action problem posed by having motivated and inspired but impotent Democrats in communities throughout the country. We can reach and connect disparate constituencies to the political process, like the unmarried women that Anna Greenberg says do not vote at rates equal to their numbers in the population but who are dispersed in the population and are not easy to target by conventional means. We can offer the meaning and purpose essential to political action to people of all backgrounds. By using the Internet to unravel the dilemmas of collective action, Democrats can become a majority political voice in this country. In the process, they might even change the nature of democracy.

Any social movement needs several elements—a shared moral purpose, leadership, rituals, a narrative about its history, and episodic moments that rejuvenate the community and create new leadership. It also needs a deep, cross-class social network supporting it, and while the Internet can enhance the other elements of a movement, it is at its most powerful in creating networks. The Internet cannot, by itself, bring magic to any organization—few would argue that the degree of creativity and excitement generated by Howard Dean's Internet campaign would have been possible with a different candidate—but it can create new social ties and solve all kinds of collective action problems. It can enable a deep and varied social network on a scale the likes of which have never before been seen.

THE LOGIC OF INTERNET COLLECTIVE ACTION

Assume for a moment that in a nation of almost 300 million people, one in every three hundred would be willing to lead a progressive cause should the opportunity present itself. This number is not as ridiculous as it may seem initially and may even be a conservative estimate when you stop to consider how naturally leaders emerge in small groups, social clubs, and informal associations. It's a fraction of the one in twenty people who once held leadership positions in civic voluntary associations in this country.[1] Assume that these people would be willing to spend a

few months leading—with all the fuss and headache that entails—a local group of Democrats interested in pushing Democratic issues in the
press, organizing local events and visibility, and talking to other people
directly about why they care about these issues. This assumption means
there are roughly a million potential short-term progressive leaders in
the United States—a wealth of largely untapped leadership potential.

Until recently, the transient nature of American society was such that
these potential leaders wouldn't know how to find fertile, continuous organizations. This is a classic case of the collective action problem, which
arises when a great number of people are willing to do something, but
only if they think it will be worthwhile because enough other people—
people they don't know—will also do it. Because of the absence of information, the rational choice for each person is not to act. They feel impotent alone. What's the point, for example, of voting for a long-shot
presidential candidate when all the polls say he is going to lose? What's
the point of sending $2 to Indonesia when such a small amount cannot
make a difference in the wake of the overwhelming devastation caused
by the tsunami? What's the point of raising your voice at a school board
meeting to vote down a bond issue when all the newspapers say it's going to be approved? Why go down to the local bar to talk about politics
when you don't know whether anyone else will be there?

As of 2000, many Americans were living in political bubbles, either
alone or with a handful of close friends, completely unaware of the extraordinary potential power they held because they had no way to communicate with like-minded others or even know that others were there.
The Internet dramatically changed this situation. As director of Internet
organizing for Howard Dean, I spent two months late in 2003 traveling
around the country visiting sixty of the nearly one thousand local Dean
community organizations. Over and over again, I heard the same idea
expressed in similar language by very different people who had volunteered their time to the campaign: "I thought I was the only one." "I
thought we were all alone." "I had no idea there were other people who
felt as strongly as I did about what was happening to our country." One
woman in rural Texas said, "I was going to divorce my husband and
move to the city, I was so lonely!"

Two things made them feel less alone. One was Dean's voice itself.
The second was the explicit awareness that at least half a million other

citizens agreed with them and were willing to commit to take action along with them. The proof was on the Dean website, on the Dean weblog, and in the thousands of local e-mail lists of Dean supporters. Its effects were transformational.

PRINCIPLES OF INTERNET-BASED COMMUNITIES

The Internet doesn't so much provide a template structure for organizing disparate individuals as it provides options heretofore unavailable to organizers. None of us on the Dean campaign knew the optimal way to organize a group, beyond the recognition that ingenuity emanating from the community itself is a critical component of effective organizing, and that rigid adherence to a single organizational approach, more than the flaws of any particular approach, will kill ingenuity quicker than anything. Jimmy Wales, the creator of Wikipedia—the online encyclopedia that anyone can edit, one of the most successful Internet architectures in history—purposefully eschews highly formalized structure and adopts a very flexible approach to Internet organization. Likewise, Craig Newmark, whose Craigslist.com hosts more than a hundred virtual communities in twenty countries, avoids strong doctrine on community architecture and responds to the unique needs of his communities. Instead of being one-size-fits-all quantitative "reputation systems," these successful projects are built on responding to a wide range of real human interactions.

That said, there are a few principles that seem to emerge repeatedly in successful large communities. These principles could be applied to a future presidential campaign, a political party, an affiliated Section 527 group—or all of these. The structure calls for a hub (the party, campaign headquarters, etc.) and edges (grassroots supporters in connected groups), relating to each other in a manner that permits the free flow of ideas between the center and the periphery and among periphery groups, ultimately resulting in the creation of many new hub groups along the periphery.

The Importance of a Hub with a Clear Moral Purpose

The strongest social structure that we can build is a networked organization with a hub or centralized structure, such as the national

Democratic Party. A strong hub works like a centralized coordinating mechanism, offering its members a shared moral purpose that gives people something to organize around. A vibrant hub can coordinate activity for the organization and perform the critically important tasks of identifying and engaging new members, who typically come to the organization through the central hub. People are unlikely to find local groups by happenstance. This speaks to the need for the hub organization to aggressively pursue new members.

Wikipedia, OhMyNews (a citizen-reporter news site), and the Dean campaign had very different hub structures, but they shared an unequivocal commitment to ideas bigger than the idea of participation alone. A meaningful, substantive core needs to develop before a large community organization can be effective.

The requirement that an online community have a clear, driving purpose dovetails with the need, widely expressed in this volume and elsewhere, for the Democratic Party to express a clear, limited, driving set of principles around which people might come together. An average of purposes is not a shared moral purpose, a list of legislative goals is not a shared moral purpose, and pandering is the opposite of purpose. Polling provides information but not a purpose. In this regard, George Lakoff's suggestions for framing the political debate need to be the final step, not the first step—the language used to communicate purpose. The opportunities available to progressives to leverage the potential of Internet organizing through the Democratic Party are predicated on the broader efforts of progressives to clearly define the purpose of the Democratic Party.

Wikipedia provides an excellent example of how hub organizers with a shared moral purpose can transfix the Internet. With two staff members, Wikipedia has become one of the top websites in the world (it recently surpassed the *New York Times* in daily hits) because it remains true to a simple, overriding idea: to build and provide a free, global encyclopedia. This goal has defined all its choices and has been more important to its organizers than the goal of getting large numbers of participants. Too often, I see Internet organizers fear that they won't grow if they make their moral purpose more important than the principle of participation. In fact, the opposite seems to be true: people aren't as likely to participate endlessly, and for no obvious, direct monetary incentive, in anything that doesn't have a goal bigger than themselves and their involvement.

Pushing Power to Edge Communities

The purpose of the hub organization should largely be to serve the end users—the citizens who empower it—in service of their shared moral purpose. The first step in serving the citizens is finding them. There are tens of millions of Americans who want a direct connection with the party or another organization. Finding them, or helping them find the party, is critical to providing them with the means to self-organize. In other words, build an enormous database, but build it as a service to the people who *want* to engage in political action.

Once the database is built, the hub can enable the desires of people at the periphery to feel powerful and engage in community action by seeding individual communities with autonomous leaders and autonomous structures that make their own decisions about how they can be most useful. Essentially, the hub is facilitating the development of many new, autonomous hubs at the periphery. Instead of imaging tens of thousands of busy ants who might be willing to send one letter or hold one house party, the hub must ensure that each one of those ants has the opportunity to become a community leader of its own group with a chance to influence the hub's decision making.

If the hub organization encourages and supports the creation of hub groups at the edges, it will generate a wealth of small, localized groups of citizens who have the capacity to organize with other Democrats, agitate, deliberate, and collectively have high-level access to party structures. These groups, in turn, will foment ideas, produce activists and candidates, raise money, perform routine campaign activities like canvassing and phone banking, and engage in highly effective word-of-mouth turnout efforts. The central group—the Democratic Party—can only solve the collective action problem if all the inspired but isolated Democrats at the periphery have autonomy from the hub to perform these activities on their own terms and in their own groups. This is the essence of hub-to-hub organizing.[2]

The influence of groups at the edges has to be meaningful. If the Democratic Party simply provides people with a means to give feedback to the central structure by rubber-stamping decisions made in Washington, then people will not engage. If the party simply regards the Internet as an unprecedented way to get people to give money—which, of course, it is—party leaders will have only learned part, and arguably not the most important part, of the Internet's organization and mobilization potential. If the hub regards the edges as servants to perform useful tasks for the central structure, Internet organizing efforts will underperform.

This may be a difficult step for an established party to take. Federated group creation and empowerment flies against conventional campaign organizing. The temptation of the hub—like any organism—is to maintain control over its component parts. Leaders of the central party organization will naturally try to maintain absolute control over its priorities and message. Some operatives are inclined to coax, lure, and drag people into political action on their terms, as Amy Sullivan, in this volume, discusses when she talks about the implied pressure placed by the congressional campaign committees on new candidates to employ a closed set of consultants in exchange for seed money. But this type of control undermines a core principle of Internet-based organizing (and, as election results have painfully demonstrated, is counterproductive for everyone but the consultants). It is hard to fight against this tendency and difficult to combat a culture that has been in place for a long time. It is also vitally *important* to do if Democrats hope to solve their collective action problem.

It may also be difficult for the central party to encourage hubs that form at the edges to continue to divide into smaller hubs, lest they become too big to be effective. Once an edge group grows large, it should focus on replicating itself to provide room for new leadership to develop. My experience in the Dean campaign suggests that optimal group size is between ten and twenty. Larger groups can create a leader/audience dynamic, with most participants assuming a passive role. Such replication can be encouraged by the core. The message from the central party to all emergent groups must constantly be: divide, divide, divide, and measure your success by how many leaders you spawn—not by how many people you lead.

ESSENTIAL ELEMENTS OF INTERNET ARCHITECTURE

The web structure itself should mimic this constant hydraulic push outward in order to tap the creative and leadership capacity of its members.

Before the Internet, it was extremely difficult to connect new people in a movement to local leaders—at minimum, it took a phone call from the central organization to local leaders. Walk through the process: someone calls Al Gore's office asking to volunteer. The volunteer coordinator then has to search a database of volunteers and give the contact information of another person in the same town, who may or may not still be active in the campaign. Furthermore, the volunteer, who might have been willing to devote many hours a week to engagement locally, will simply be pigeonholed as a "donor" or a "phone banker" to be used, at most, for twenty hours in a last-minute phone banking push.

With a website and especially with e-mail, the task is much easier and more efficient. With a website, you can easily list locations and contact information in a central place and actively direct people to local events. With e-mail, you can redirect national inquiries to local leaders, who can help local volunteers develop into active strategists and organizers.

For a continuous community to work on a mechanical level, it needs to exist both online and offline. An easily accessed online presence must facilitate online communication and regularly scheduled offline meetings, with leadership opportunities available to people in both settings. The effort needs to be simple, so that people everywhere can easily search for and find others with similar interests who want to communicate or organize in similar ways. If properly structured, online communication tools should afford opportunities for cross-fertilization and real-world connections among otherwise isolated individuals.

Because every community is different, each will need and want to work with its own set of online tools, and it is naive to think it is possible to predict beforehand the most suitable tools for a community. Internet consultants, myself included, come with strong opinions and may be biased toward certain structures, although we only know as much as our specific experience has taught us. From my experience, the items I discuss below—meeting tools, listservs, and blogs—would be useful for the organizational purposes that could best serve the political interests of progressives.

Meeting Tools

If you buy into the hub-to-hub model, the key to creating a strong party is cultivating tens of thousands of continuous offline communities:

groups of people who meet in person on a regular basis. The Dean campaign depended heavily on the commercial website Meetup.com as a simple tool for organizing regular offline meetings of volunteers. Meetup.com made it easy for people to find each other and facilitated virtual organizing of in-person gatherings. Designed as a nonpolitical site that enables people with similar interests to find each other online and to meet offline, Meetup.com houses a large database of public places that are willing to host meetings of like-minded people, along with simple web tools to enable people to search for others in their vicinity with similar interests.

When the Dean campaign utilized Meetup.com in 2003, it didn't impose a fee on organizers or require participants to agree in advance to organize a meeting—it simply matched like-minded people with each other, arranged a fixed meeting time, and assigned a suitable host venue. Meetup.com has since imposed these restrictions, which are impediments to the formation of small groups, but an organization like the Democratic Party could provide the service that Meetup.com supplied the Dean campaign by developing, maintaining, and understanding how to use the relevant databases and ensuring that groups can form without the predicate of a preselected leader.

Party leaders must first absorb the value of meeting tools and understand how easy it is to develop them properly. On a mechanical level, a good meeting tool has several characteristics. An icon identifying the meeting tool should be easily identifiable from a central site, like the top part of the party's home page, and it should appear regularly on e-mail the party sends out.[3] The database of gathering places should be populated with public sites—bars and restaurants and parks—as people are more likely to be intimidated by gatherings held in unfamiliar private homes. The public locations in the database should be easy to find. Meetings should be held on a regular day and at a regular time, and they should be ongoing, making it easy and natural for people to attend at their convenience and to make attending part of their usual routine. They should be monthly at least, but ideally weekly, so you are never more than a few days away from dropping in on a group of like-minded people.[4]

This model emphasizes simplicity, so that people everywhere can easily search for and find others with similar interests who want to communicate or organize in similar ways. With good meeting tools, people in similar localities can build local political structures and facilitate most of the communication with their members. This is less an Internet function than a cultural one, and we have great models for it from the Knights of Pythias to the Rotary Club to the PTA, all federated organizations that make it very easy to start local chapters.

Listservs

On the Dean campaign, more than four hundred of about a thousand local groups built committees themselves—many developing out of Meetup.com and other meeting tools we developed. Although there was some variation in how they approached community-building, the common thread among their efforts was the use of listservs as a communication and organizing tool.

A listserv is an automatic mailing list that transmits e-mail messages to everyone in its database. On their own initiative, grassroots supporters developed Dean listservs in all fifty states and thousands of communities (there were nearly a thousand Dean Yahoo listservs, and countless numbers on other services), which provided a powerful communication infrastructure for developing and sharing ideas. Because all listserv communications are shared instantly with everyone on the list, anyone with a question or an idea can broadcast it to everyone else, permitting others to broadcast their reactions and responses to the entire community in a manner that facilitates brainstorming, creative thinking, and problem solving. For instance, the groups Georgia for Dean and Philly for Dean developed reputations for having outstanding committee structures through listserv discussions of committee organizing, leading people in other groups to contact them for advice and guidance. Ideas spread virally through listservs, empowering local supporters across the country to build a strong campaign infrastructure without guidance from headquarters. The Seattle Dean listserv planned a "flyering on tax day" campaign and sent a note to the New York for Dean listserv to ask for design ideas. One man on the Georgia for Dean's listserv suggested a business card for Dean to pass out, and another man quickly responded that he would design one. Ideas that used to die over the breakfast table became real.

The power of listservs is that they make it possible to engage numerous supporters in multiple initiatives that would not emerge from traditional campaign models of centralized control. The largest database in the world doesn't allow for people to connect locally or to pursue original ideas rather than ideas pushed from above.

Blogs

The Dean weblog was perhaps the most visible tool to people outside the campaign. Because it received a fair amount of media attention, "Blog for America" became a symbol of the high-tech revolution in political campaigning. To its core users, the blog was a place to receive news and share feedback about the protracted struggle of running for president.

The Dean blog was a vital, pulsing, storytelling hub, where campaign staff (and sometimes the candidate) pulled back the curtain on what was going on inside the campaign. We thought of it as an ongoing staff meeting, the place where the entire campaign could come together. Other institutions, such as the Democratic Party or 527 groups, can also create a vibrant hub blog. The key is that it should be close to the heartbeat of the organization rather than an extension of the communications department of a campaign or group, where press releases are dressed up in slightly looser language. A successful organizational blog expresses the needs and character of an organization, permitting people to engage beyond talking points.

What I found most compelling on the blog was the way people would share their stories of offline involvement—people who had found a deep sense of empowerment because of things they had accomplished in their communities. It is a free-ranging way to share ideas, but a very fertile one because it is so open. Logic might suggest that we should compartmentalize action, expression, needs, and emotion into different buckets—a forum for the politicos, a forum for the activists, a forum for those who write political poetry—but the magic of the blog stems from the jumble of these together.

PULLING IT ALL TOGETHER

These mechanical principles of Internet organizing are best understood in human terms. The best Internet organizers don't start with technology. They start with purpose and human nature.

When I design software with a team or a community, we assume that people *want* to have power over their lives and improve the world for others, that people *want* to connect in communities, and that there are *millions* of potential Democratic leaders in this country that simply don't have a venue for their leadership skills. We begin with the expectation that our software and the way it is deployed will enable those pent-up human needs, and then refine what we build by discerning the exact nature of what users need by listening to their feedback.

The end result of this approach, and the working result of the Internet organizational model, is a vast, robust, trustworthy, structured set of communities where people share the joys and struggles of personal interaction that ideally should be at the root of all political activity. The glories of friendship, the small power struggles, the smell, look, and feel of rooms cramped with a bunch of determined people—these are the things that give purpose to politics. It is politics in human terms on a human scale. And it is the type of involvement progressives need in order to engage the Democratic Party as a vehicle for effective political action.

In human terms, this means I should be able to go online to the national or my local Democratic Party website, or any number of affiliated sites, and in a short period of time find a place where I can meet other enthusiastic people and assume an aggressive leadership role in a grassroots activity. This is starting to happen because the Democratic Party is working on it. A successful initiative will require a lot of work and innovation on the part of groups inside and outside the party structure. Right now, it is easier to get involved in a progressive political community through affiliated groups like Drinking Liberally or Democracy for America than through the Democratic Party, whose initial entry into the Internet world was oriented toward fund-raising and message dissemination rather than organizing. It will require a change in thinking by party leaders and staff to recognize that encouraging real or virtual local organization is the most important role the Internet can play.

The party, 527 groups, and local political organizations with an online presence should join forces to build a database of meeting places to rival Meetup.com for the purpose of organizing every precinct in the country. At a fraction of the cost of one consultant, these progressive hub organizations would be wise to invest in two dozen web-savvy twenty-year-olds to find and call local restaurants and cafes and book-stores around the country that are willing to host meetings of Democrats. Then it should take that database, make it public, and create a ritualistic monthly or weekly time for meetings in those places.

With a "Meet" icon prominently displayed on every affiliated website, organizational opportunities could be promoted widely to potential members with the message from the hub along the lines of: "If you meet, we will enable you to be powerful through collective, coordinated action. If you meet, we will be able to hear you—speaking as a group—and incorporate your needs into our platform. If you meet, you'll have fun, and you'll see how incredibly satisfying and social politics can be."

Imagine what could have happened had the Democratic Party attempted to do this during the last presidential cycle. In June 2004, John Kerry used his website and two-million-person e-mail list to advertise highly targeted, one-time events, while dropping the link to Meetup.com from his website and halting coordinated activities with local groups unless group leaders had been vetted. The campaign had developed a first-rate meeting tool, which activists used for all kinds of public and private events, but the structure of the tool encouraged people to use it more for events in private homes than public places. The campaign never created its own ritual meetings nor built its own database of places where people could meet. In other words, while using the extraordinary power of the Internet for mass projects and mass fundraising, the Kerry campaign largely behaved like other campaigns before it, maintaining centralized control over operations and endorsing hierarchy at nearly every level.

If a future campaign or the Democratic Party—operating with a list as large as Kerry's—were to focus its communications on enabling easy weekly meetings, it could build an unprecedented mobilization structure that would surpass in effectiveness the highly successful efforts developed by affiliated groups such as America Coming Together. With the goal of empowering a group of engaged citizens in every precinct in the country, it will be possible come Election Day to rely on a person-to-person mobilization network that will be unsurpassed in its reach. To do so will require appreciating the organizing potential of the Internet and letting go of the old habits of centralized command and control, while maintaining a hub as a conduit and coordinating mechanism. This is understandably a difficult step for traditional campaign consultants and party officials to take. But it is the most critical one to take if progressives are going to unlock the organizing potential of the Internet.

NOTES

1. Theda Skocpol, *Diminished Democracy: From Membership to Management in American Civic Life* (Norman: University of Oklahoma Press, 2003).

2. There are a few examples of successful hub-to-hub Internet organizing, including Wikipedia, Democracy for America, Drinking Liberally, and Music for America. In each of these, the organizational focus and the metrics of organizational success rest with the number and spread of vibrant local groups rather than the numbers of individuals.

3. This may seem obvious, but you'd be surprised how many campaigns and organizations think that building a tool is more important than advertising it. It is not uncommon for campaign staff to battle fiercely over what to place in the top upper-right and upper-left corners of their websites. Typically, advocates of placing a "donate," "watch this video," or "send this particular letter" button win such battles. I'm suggesting that these buttons should take second fiddle to the "meet" button for a while.

4. The more frequent a meeting, the less it becomes a lecture and the more it becomes a fertile space for action and productive organizing—and, critically, the more acceptable it becomes to be a casual group member. Like church or a weekly poker game, politics will work the best when it is highly normalized and casual.

12

BLOGGING FOR POLITICAL CHANGE

Chris Bowers

It was at a local bar in December 2003 when I first suggested to my brother Andy that popular progressive bloggers, such as Markos Moulitsas Zuniga of Daily Kos and Atrios, the pseudonym of the blogger who runs the website Eschaton, might just be the Jack Kerouacs and Allen Ginsbergs of our generation. To be sure, this was something of an intentional overstatement, the sort of claim one makes at a bar in order to start a spirited conversation. However, it was a claim I am willing to partially defend, since I believe it provides an opening toward an improved understanding of political weblogs, or blogs.

To understand why, consider the similarities between political blogs and avant-garde art, which I once studied when my career ambition was to become an English professor. While the term "avant-garde poetry" might generate associations with pretentious, incomprehensible gobbledygook, those artists properly known as "avant-garde" shared two important characteristics unrelated to the content of their work:

1. Avant-garde "movements" (there are no avant-garde individuals—just collectives) have always created counterinstitutions for the production, judgment, distribution, and consumption of art. These

"counterinstitutions" operate independently from established institutions for the production, judgment, distribution, and consumption of aesthetic-based art.[1]
2. The purpose of these counterinstitutions has been to relocate the
   primary purpose of art away from an aesthetic function toward
   something transformative. However, since there have been so
   many manifestations of the avant-garde, the desired alternative to
   the aesthetic function has varied greatly.[2]

There is a striking similarity between these characteristics of avant-
garde art and blogging, which served as the basis for the claim I made
to Andy about the similarity between bloggers and avant-garde artists
such as Ginsberg and Kerouac. The various avant-garde movements of
the past century (and there are probably close to one hundred), produced their own journals, ran their own theaters, wrote their own criticism, made their own publicity, developed their own audiences, generated their own networks, became their own editors, solicited their own
projects, bought their own printing materials, secured their own gallery
space, ran their own bookstores, and, in short, developed full-fledged
artistic counterinstitutions (even artistic countereconomies). In fact,
many movements developed counterinstitutions that were so strong that
the movements became internationally famous (the Beats, Language
poets, dada, Surrealists, etc.).

Similarly, in reaction to the mainstream media, the progressive political blogosphere (a blogosphere is a network of blogs) has developed
into a full-fledged counterinstitution for the production, judgment, distribution, and consumption of political writing. We are our own editors,
publishers, and publicists. We create our own websites, pay for many of
our own servers and bandwidth, develop our own networks, and even
hold our own award competitions. In addition to on-site reporting from
countless local and statewide events, we produce original, on-site reporting from major events such as the Iraq war and national political
conventions. We develop original research on polling information and
political strategy. We interview leading figures in American politics and
even have live, open-ended conversations with them on our blogs. In
short, we have created an entire underground world of political news
that operates independently of established, mainstream institutions of
political journalism.

Creating a counterinstitution is only half of being avant-garde, however. The various manifestations of the artistic avant-garde also sought to relocate the primary purpose of art away from its aesthetic function. Again, we can find a clear analogy to the blogosphere. While it is generally understood that the purpose of established institutions of political journalism is primarily to inform (and, usually, to make a profit in so doing), political blogging strives to relocate the primary purpose of political and opinion journalism in agitation toward action.

THE FUNCTION OF DISCOURSE

In the spring of 2004, after two years of reading and posting on blogs, I became a blogger myself. In late April, I secured gigs projecting the presidential election at David Nir's Swing State Project (www .swingstateproject.com) and as a full-time blogger at Jerome Armstrong's My Due Diligence (www.mydd.com), where I still write full-time. By late September 2004, I had gained some notoriety for raising money for Ginny Schrader's congressional campaign in Pennsylvania's Eighth District and for arguing that several polling organizations, especially Gallup, were including too many Republicans in their public opinion surveys of the presidential election.[3]

Around the time I was helping to make waves for alleging bias in Gallup's polling samples, partisan conservative blogs were bathing in praise and publicity from the mainstream media to a degree blogs had never before experienced. Conservative bloggers had "forced" CBS to admit that it could not verify the authenticity of the documents it had used in a story about President Bush's time in the Texas Air National Guard. Not since the heyday of Howard Dean's presidential campaign in late 2003 had political blogs been the subject of so much attention from mainstream news. By all accounts, the attention lavished upon conservative blogs for breaking this story remains the high watermark of mainstream legitimization of political blogging.

During this frenzy, one particular article about blogging in the mainstream media stood out, if for no other reason than the fact that it was the only one written by an actual blogger. For some time, Billmon, the pseudonym for the blogger of Whiskey Bar (http://billmon.org), was widely regarded as one of the best writers, possibly the very best, in the progressive political blogosphere. On September 26, 2004, Billmon published an op-ed in the *Los Angeles Times* about blogging. In Billmon's formulation, by September 2004, blogs had already sold out:

> By most accounts, blogs—web logs to the uninitiated—scored a major coup last week when CBS News admitted that it couldn't vouch for the authenticity of memos supposedly written by George W. Bush's commander in the Texas Air National Guard. The conservative bloggers who led the charge against the CBS story were hailed as giant slayers. And yet it's the blogging phenomenon itself that may need the last rites.
>
> That may seem a strange thing to say, given the flattering coverage of blogs triggered by the CBS affair. But the media's infatuation has a distinct odor of the deathbed about it—not for the blogosphere, which has a commercially bright future, but for the idea of blogging as a grass-roots challenge to the increasingly sanitized "content" peddled by the Time Warner–Capital Cities–Disney–General Electric–Viacom–Tribune media oligopoly.[4]

For Billmon, the importance of the political blogosphere is its superior, challenging, subversive content. He praised the "articulate, querulous and sometimes profane *voices* from the Internet hinterland" that filled his blog with comments, together creating a *"culture* of dissent."[5] Comparing blogging to forms of aesthetic or cultural expression, Billmon wrote:

> America has always had a knack for absorbing, and taming, its cultural revolutionaries. The rise and long, sad fall of rock 'n' roll is probably the most egregious example, while the music industry's colonization of rap is a more recent one.[6]

Billmon's emphasis is on voice, culture, speech, conversation, and content. In his formulation, the primary divergence between the blogosphere and existing media is aesthetic and stylistic. For Billmon, blogs provide a populist, subversive, and edgy outlet for discussion and contemplation of real issues, while the arrogant media oligopoly slowly moves toward the production of more and more sanitized, safe, and content-free discourse.

This is a view of the blogosphere I do not share and have never shared. For me, the primary difference between the blogosphere and the media oligopoly is not the content and register of our discourse but the function of that discourse. While journalists in the media oligopoly work to inform (at which many in the blogosphere would argue they do a terrible job), we work to agitate. While most journalists labor toward objectivity, we clearly labor toward subjectivity, agency, and direct political action. The purpose is not to create an alternative avenue for edgy discursive expression, although that clearly has happened. Instead, it is about organizing and effectively channeling the activism of the people who take part in and witness those discussions.

I do not wish to single out Billmon when it comes to what I feel is a misdirected focus on the stylistic differences between the mainstream media and blogging. On this front, he is hardly alone. I quoted him here in part to correct what I feel is an unfortunate tendency of established journalists, pundits, and columnists to discuss the nature of blogging without asking for much input on the subject from actual bloggers. The most typical, and frustrating, example of this is the long-running habit of journalists to decry the amorality of bloggers and their seeming disregard for journalistic ethics. This is a discussion that dates back at least to February 2004, when the *Columbia Journalism Review*'s Campaign Desk criticized Daily Kos for publishing the early afternoon exit polls in the New Hampshire primary.[7] Since that time, hundreds of similar arguments have been made by many established news organizations. There was even a conference on "Blogging, Journalism, and Credibility" at Harvard in January 2005, to which only one actual blogger who operates entirely outside of the mainstream media was invited to attend.[8] In what for my money is the most extreme example of journalists decrying the lack of morality on blogs, my blogging partner, Jerome Armstrong, was even accused of causing the stock market to drop dramatically on November 2, 2004, after becoming the first blogger to post the early state-by-state exit polls of the presidential election![9]

To argue that blogs are either outlets for edgy and subversive content or dens of amoral, unaccountable journalism is to assume that the primary difference between bloggers and journalists is stylistic rather than purposive. Both critiques of blogs assume that bloggers are working primarily to achieve the same goals as journalists, which is to inform. Both critiques argue that what differentiates blogging from journalism is the bloggers' subversive style. However, considering just what stories have actually made blogs famous, I feel that it should be rather obvious that blogs are becoming famous not for their antiestablishment views or their

amoral brand of journalism but for justifiably claiming real political accomplishments. Conservative bloggers had helped turn the nationwide
discussion of a story that was potentially damaging to President Bush into
a story about how the media was being unfair to President Bush. Progressive bloggers had received significant mainstream media attention in
late 2002 for helping to remove Trent Lott from his leadership position in
the Senate over his specious remarks at the late Sen. Strom Thurmond's
(R-S.C.) 100th birthday party. In 2003, bloggers were frequently covered
by the press for assisting in the meteoric rise of Howard Dean's presidential campaign. Last year, I had begun to achieve a certain amount of notoriety for calling Gallup's methodology into question. More recent
achievements of progressive blogs include outing Jeff Gannon as a
pseudo-journalist within the White House Press gaggle, helping to elect
Howard Dean chairman of the Democratic National Committee, serving
as Democratic Party whips during the Social Security debate, and bringing underdog Democrat Paul Hackett to the brink of victory in a special
congressional election in one of Ohio's most conservative districts.[10] Every
single time the mainstream media has paid significant attention to the activity of bloggers, it is not for the style and content of what we write, but
instead for what we have helped to agitate or accomplish.

This is not a coincidence. Blogs have received the most attention from
the mainstream media for their political accomplishments because the
purpose of blogging is to bring about political change. Conversations on
blogs are more akin to conversations at meetings for activist, political organizations than to conversations in coffee shops. This is the true way in
which blogs are different from mainstream journalism. While traditionally journalists have worked to inform, bloggers strive to relocate the primary purpose of journalism in direct, partisan political action. Blogs are
not just political journalism with a different style: they are political journalism with a different purpose.

TAKING ACTION

Once the action-oriented nature of progressive blogs is understood,
their awesome potential in helping dedicated progressives form a new
governing majority in America can also be understood. As of May 1,
2005, the sixty most trafficked progressive blogs that run advertisements

through the Blogads.com advertising service received nearly 10 million page views per week.[11] This translates into roughly 1.5 million different people visiting and reading this group of progressive blogs every weekday, a number comparable to the daily American audience for CNN.[12] Furthermore, according to a reader survey conducted by Blogads.com a few months earlier, nearly 80 percent of political blog readers who self-identify as Democrats contributed to a Democratic political campaign in 2004,[13] compared to 15 percent of the population as a whole.[14] One can expect that compared to the general population, equally disproportionate percentages of progressive blog readers engage in a range of civic and political action, including volunteering to work for Democratic campaigns, attending party and campaign events, and writing or calling members of the media and political officials.

Clearly, the dedication and activism of the progressive blogosphere has not been diluted by its still-growing size. In this book, Zephyr Teachout talks about how the Internet can solve the collective action problem associated with organizing unrelated people, arguing that the greatest potential for the Internet rests with identifying and creating grassroots leaders and mobilizing large numbers of people through interpersonal action initiated online. The blogosphere can be and should be a component of the organizing potential of the Internet, helping to organize unrelated people into taking all levels of political activism. This includes those who are only able to participate in thirty-second activities, such as signing a petition, as well as identifying those who can become well-trained, full-time ward leaders and regional coordinators. Most importantly, the progressive blogosphere reaches a deeply committed group of people who can be counted on for all manner of political activity. This is an awesome reservoir of potential progressive political activism that to date has not been seriously tapped by established institutions of progressive power, including the Democratic Party and allied, issue-advocacy organizations.

ORGANIZING THE DEMOCRATIC PARTY FROM THE NETROOTS AND ORGANIZING THE NETROOTS FOR THE DEMOCRATIC PARTY

As a result of the rapid growth of the progressive blogosphere, the community of progressive bloggers is diffuse and disorganized. As recently as

July 2003, when Howard Dean first rode blogs to prominence, the readership of the progressive blogosphere was less than one-tenth of what is it today,[15] and at the time it even lagged behind the readership of the conservative blogosphere (now it is nearly 50 percent larger).[16] Even the oldest progressive blogs, such as Josh Marshall's Talking Points Memo, have yet to reach their fifth birthday, and thus there are few preexisting institutional structures to facilitate organization.[17] Furthermore, because progressive blogs tend to have been created intentionally as new mechanisms for the distribution and dissemination of political discourse, their strong independent streak makes it difficult to organize them along traditional models. The progressive blogosphere will never become a mass-member civic organization that operates according to the same structures as the League of Women Voters or the American Legion. Its structure will always be far looser, its hierarchy will be much more difficult to determine, and the location and meeting habits of its members will always be far more disparate.

This is not to imply, however, either that the progressive blogosphere cannot be better organized or that it lacks consensus issues around which it can be organized. One particularly important area of consensus is partisan self-identification among progressive blog participants. Roughly 90 percent of the traffic on progressive blogs occurs on blogs that self-identity as Democratic.[18] Democratic self-identification is thus a common, uniting thread of the progressive blogosphere that could potentially be used to help organize the political blogosphere.

Considering this, no institution is better situated to help participate in this organization, and thus reap the potential activist benefits of the progressive blogosphere, than the Democratic Party itself. Already, some members of the leadership of the party have engaged blogs in a variety of ways, but as I will describe below, to date that engagement is spotty. To truly engage the blogosphere, the leadership of the Democratic Party must do so on a far more regular and widespread basis and must do so in ways that take into account the internal workings and cultural norms of the blogosphere. Below are four particularly useful ways that Democrats could help to organize the blogosphere, and vice versa.

Increase Two-Way Communication

Community interaction between bloggers, commenters, and readers has been one of the defining traits of the progressive blogosphere. In addition to sending out daily talking points and press releases to bloggers via e-mail, the leadership of the Democratic Party should be willing to be questioned by bloggers on a regular basis. Just as the Democratic Party leadership holds a weekly conference call with members of the media, this would require a weekly conference call between bloggers and a leading Democratic Party figure in the House, Senate, Democratic National Committee, or Democratic Governor's Association. Currently, conference calls between bloggers and leading Democrats are both rare and irregular.

Furthermore, while many Democratic senators, representatives, and party officials have taken to directly posting articles on progressive blogs, these elected officials rarely, if ever, respond to the questions posted in the comments section by those who read their posts. Although this would certainly be a time-consuming activity, it is important for Democratic Party officials to increase their degree of interaction with members of the blog community, as blog communities thrive on interaction. To post and not respond is the blog equivalent of ringing a doorbell, leaving a note, and running away.

Joint Promotion

Another hallmark of the progressive blogosphere is that the many progressive blogs promote one another, helping to foster a wider community. Frequently, when one blog links to another blog, the link will be returned and a mutually supportive relationship will develop. Also, many bloggers form "blog rings," where the mutual exchange of information takes place among several blogs simultaneously.

Currently, a couple of leading Democratic officials send out daily press releases via e-mail to several leading bloggers as a means of helping to distribute the Democratic message to the party grass roots. However, the party does very little in return for this publicity. One particularly useful thing the party could do to promote the progressive blogosphere would be to create a "Blog News" page that would serve to aggregate and organize discussions in the blogosphere along the lines of

Google News. If it were of the same quality as Google News and could successfully sort articles posted on pro-Democratic blogs by topic, it would almost instantly become an extremely popular and integral part of the progressive blogosphere. This would create a healthy, mutually beneficial, and vastly increased exchange of reader traffic between the Democratic Party's website and the progressive blogosphere.

Ask for More than Just Money

While much has been made of the success of online fund-raising by presidential campaigns in the 2004 cycle, progressive bloggers often feel that this is the only source of action for which most leaders in the Democratic Party find blogs useful. The typical complaint is that bloggers feel they are treated like "ATM machines" and that the party does not take the many other forms of activism we regularly undertake seriously.

This could be remedied, however, if all local Democratic Party events and actions around the country were gathered into a single database, searchable by date and zip code, so that users could find out what was going on in their area every day of the week. Furthermore, it should be possible to allow individual Democrats to submit and organize their own local, grassroots events and actions with this database. It would not be difficult to develop safeguards to make certain that every event and action has a contact person and that no phony events are submitted. This potentially would bring a huge new wave of volunteers into the party and would show the progressive blogosphere that their activist skills are valued as much as their wallets.

Twenty-Four Hours a Day, Seven Days a Week

Another hallmark of the most successful progressive blogs is that they are constantly posting new information. For example, my blog—MyDD—posted more than 2,000 original front-page articles and 4,500 contributor-written articles on the "diaries" page in 2004. On Daily Kos, more than 5,000 new articles were posted on the front page and more than 75,000 articles on the "diaries" page in 2004. One of the reasons that the blogosphere continues to grow is that it never shuts down and is always abuzz with activity. Considering this, the Democratic Party should hire at least four full-time bloggers for its own blog, Kicking Ass, to make certain that there is always a wealth of content to guarantee that people keep coming back. There is no reason why the Democratic Party blog cannot have a level of content equal to or greater than every progressive blog in the country.

MUTUAL BENEFITS BETWEEN PARTY AND BLOGS

Recognizing the enormous activist potential of progressive blogs and understanding how to coordinate with members of the progressive blogosphere could go a long way toward helping to revitalize positive volunteer activism in the Democratic Party. The key to accomplishing this goal lies in understanding that the progressive blogosphere is more than just a collection of subversive journalists and more than just a large ATM. It also lies in understanding the social and cultural norms of the blogosphere, which is a large counteruniverse of political news and activism. If the Democratic Party can help organize the activist avant-garde of the Democratic Party's rank and file, then the activist avant-garde of the Democratic Party's rank and file will help to organize the Democratic Party exponentially in return. Embrace the avant-garde, and it will embrace you back.

NOTES

1. The idea of artistic counterinstitutions is based largely upon Libbie Rifkin, *Career Moves: Olson, Creeley, Zukofsky, Berrigan, and the American Avant-Garde* (Madison: University of Wisconsin Press, 2000).

2. This idea is based largely upon Peter Burger, *Theory of the Avant-Garde*, trans. Jochen Schulte-Sasse (St. Paul: University of Minnesota Press, 1984).

3. My work on this subject was aided greatly by Ruy Teixeira of Donkey Rising (http://www.emergingdemocraticmajorityweblog.com/donkeyrising/); Steve Soto of the Left Coaster (http://www.theleftcoaster.com/); and DemfromCT of the Next Hurrah (http://thenexthurrah.typepad.com/the_next_hurrah/). It eventually resulted in advertising from MoveOn.org.

4. Billmon, "Blogging Sells, and Sells Out," *Los Angeles Times*, September 26, 2004.

5. Billmon, "Blogging Sells, and Sells Out," emphasis mine.

6. Billmon, "Blogging Sells, and Sells Out."

7. For more discussion on this topic, see Jay Rosen, "The Morals Squad at *CJR's* Campaign Desk," PressThink, February 17, 2004, http://journalism.nyu.edu/pubzone/weblogs/pressthink/2004/02/17/campaign_desk.html.

8. The home page for the conference can be found at http://cyber.law.harvard.edu/webcred.

9. One such report can be found at http://www.internetnews.com/bus-news/article.php/3430481, although the story inaccurately cited the Drudge Report, not MyDD, as the first blog to publish the data.

10. For a useful summary of recent blog accomplishments, plus an example of the journalistic ethics argument, see Adam Cohen, "The Latest Rumblings in the Blogosphere: Questions about Ethics," *New York Times*, May 8, 2005.

11. Statistics from Blogads.com (http://blogads.com).

12. As of May 10, 2005, CNN's daily American audience was estimated at 1.74 million, according to LostRemote.com at http://www.lostremote.com/archives/000806.html.

13. Statistics from http://www.blogads.com/survey/blog_reader_survey.html.

14. "Voters Liked Campaign 2004, but Too Much 'Mud Slinging,'" Pew Research Center for the People and the Press, November 11, 2004, available at http://people-press.org/reports/display.php3?ReportID=233.

15. These figures are based on a study of blog traffic conducted by Outside the Beltway on July 27, 2003, and posted at http://www.outsidethebeltway.com/archives/002648.html.

16. Based on my own regular updates of Blog Traffic at MyDD.

17. New organizations, such as BlogPac.org, are trying to remedy this situation.

18. Source: Blogads.com.

Conclusion

BLUEPRINT FOR A PROGRESSIVE ERA

Matthew R. Kerbel

Political failure is supposed to breed recrimination and name-calling, and the national Democratic Party has amassed an impressive record of political failure over the past generation. John Kerry's defeat—at the hands of a president viewed by many progressives as highly vulnerable— could have resulted in outright warfare among Democrats whose feelings remained raw from the bruising and impassioned primary campaign that consumed most of 2003. Instead, establishment and newer Democrats have been unified in their commitment to move past their devastating losses of 2004.

The voices expressed in this book, from Beltway insiders to grassroots activists and from political practitioners to academics to journalists, demonstrate extraordinary consensus about what progressives need to do to reclaim the political advantage they have lost to conservatives in order to get off what E. J. Dionne descriptively calls the "road to nowhere." As George Lakoff writes, it is remarkable how much progressives agree on. That consensus emanates from the shared observation that progressives already know who they are and what they stand for, which must serve as a basis for what they say and how they say it.

Party elites and grassroots supporters together need to:

- Claim the mantle of a proud progressive tradition rooted in the values of fairness, global leadership, and community
- Embrace conviction, but distinguish it from required orthodoxy, and remember that conviction projects strength
- Recognize that disagreements over policy priorities are inevitable and healthy and need not conflict with the development of a progressive message based in principle
- Craft the language of political discourse in a clear, direct manner with a message rooted in progressive values and a long history of progressive accomplishments

At the same time, each needs to address challenges to doing business as usual, in order to:

- Have the strength to confront entrenched party interests when they stand in the way of advancing progressives' political prospects
- Have the courage to ease away from centralized control of grassroots organizing by campaigns and hub institutions like the Democratic National Committee, and the wisdom to appreciate how to maximize the organizational power of the Internet
- Embrace the potential of weblogs to instigate political action and the political value of electing candidates beholden to the money and labor of ordinary individuals

If progressives are able to do this, we will begin to present a strong, principled, and effective face to voters who will be ready to look at us anew. As Alan Abramowitz explains, progressives are not as deep in the political wilderness as conventional wisdom suggests. George W. Bush won a narrow victory as an incumbent in an environment where enough people—notably a small group of security-conscious swing voters—who otherwise disliked his policy agenda believed he would keep them safe. Despite fervent beliefs among progressives about Bush's vulnerabilities, his reelection was the most likely outcome in 2004, with the most notable aspect of his performance being how badly Bush did compared to other incumbents of the last century. It falls to Democrats to make the critically important case that they can compete with Republicans on security matters, but they will now have the opportunity to do this without having to face an incumbent whose greatest advantage was lingering memories of the days following September 11, 2001.

Progressives may also have the luxury of making this case in a favorable political climate. Republican National Committee chair Ken Mehlman is correct when he says, "The Republican Party is in a stronger position today than at any time since the Great Depression"—as a party in government, where they run everything. The situation with the electorate is another matter. Attention to an agenda centered on Terri Schiavo's feeding tube, judicial nominations, and the status of Social Security thirty years hence, coupled with soaring gas prices and a tragically bungled response to Hurricane Katrina, left supermajorities of voters feeling the nation was veering badly off course during the first year of Bush's second term. The early months of 2005 are of course light-years removed from the midterm elections of 2006, but the early trends should raise eyebrows among leaders of both parties.

AN UNSUSTAINABLE POLITICAL MOMENT

This is because we live in an era of sharply drawn partisan distinctions that cannot persist indefinitely and that threaten to collapse under the weight of a Republican agenda that seeks to impose dramatic changes on slender majorities. Despite the closeness of the vote in the last three national election cycles and despite the narrow margins by which Republicans have held the White House, the House of Representatives, and until recently the Senate, the Bush administration has methodically advanced an agenda that without hyperbole can be described as revolutionary, as he seeks to cement a long-term era of Republican political dominance.

Prior to the Bush administration, Republican presidents dating back to Nixon kept their strongest partisans happy with rhetoric and key symbolic actions while reaching across the aisle to govern. This is the way the political system is designed to work, and it is how it works during ordinary times. Bush has inverted this governing model, offering the rhetoric of "compassionate conservatism" to centrist voters while pursuing an agenda backed by his core supporters. This governing approach is extraordinary and suits a period of monumental change.

In the way he has campaigned and governed, George W. Bush has departed from the conservative orthodoxy of every Republican nominee from Nixon through Dole, each of whom acknowledged the social welfare state while attempting to shift the balance of power from Washington to the states. From Nixon's block grants to Reagan's tax cuts to the Republican "Contract With America," a libertarian streak runs through this period of Republican governance, a reliance on the self and a belief in localism tempered by a reluctant acceptance that, Bill Clinton's famous pronouncement notwithstanding, the era of Big Government is hardly over.

Bush is different. His brand of conservatism enlists the national government in the service of the well-to-do. It accepts a merger of government and corporate interests that rejects the social welfare state and, indeed, seeks to undo it. It invokes God as a rationale for policy making, blurring the line between church and state. Although some Republicans who came before him may have privately supported these objectives in full or in part, none had the temerity to attempt to implement them as policy or the inclination to ignore the political center and govern and campaign to the base.

It is possible to find in this behavior a parallel to the decline of the Democratic Party as a dominant force in the 1960s. After thirty years of winning presidential elections and legislative majorities, Democrats began to abandon proactive opportunity-based government in favor of an outcome-centered platform that excited key constituent groups but did not speak to the mainstream. Republicans deftly exploited this shift by associating Democrats with a host of out-groups, notably Eastern, secular, intellectual, and Hollywood elites, along with, in an effective appeal to the uglier side of human nature, Reagan's stereotypical "welfare queens," gays, antiwar youth, the sexually tolerant, civil rights supporters, and whatever group could be easily demonized. Indeed, the term "liberal" has been so effectively branded as Godless, weak, and anti-American that today's liberals are wise to rally around the term "progressive" to define a new brand of liberal politics.

The parallel to Bush conservatism is that, like post-1960s liberalism, it plays best with groups that are among the party's most energized supporters—in this case, corporate and religious groups—but it risks alienating the center, to say nothing of fiscal conservatives and libertarians still operating under the Republican umbrella. Were it to play out in a similar fashion, the conservative movement as we know it will begin to become unhinged, leaving Democrats with an opening to demonize the excesses of conservatism while presenting a competing vision of American society. Of course, Bush is banking on being able to forge a political realignment that will allow Republicans to consolidate their recent gains and function as a majority party in a new political system reminiscent of the pre–New Deal Republican Party. There is no way to know which way things will play out, although the present instability in the political system offers progressives an opportunity to define the next political era on our terms—if we are aware of the political stakes and if we can move effectively to capitalize on the instability that revolutionary regimes invariably create.

THINKING BEYOND FIFTY-PERCENT-PLUS-ONE

Until recently, it wasn't at all clear that progressives understood the magnitude of the situation. During the first Bush term, congressional Democrats operated under business-as-usual assumptions, attempting to find middle ground with congressional Republicans and the administration only to find more often than not that their efforts at compromise were swatted away. Democratic incumbents who sought to work with the administration were nonetheless targeted for defeat by a Republican Party seeking victory everywhere it could be had. Grassroots Democrats arguably recognized the lethal tactics of today's Republican Party more quickly than their Beltway brethren and came to regard compromise by Democrats as a kind of spinelessness—a key factor in the meteoric rise of Howard Dean's presidential campaign in 2003. By 2005, when the agenda shifted to the elimination of the Social Security safety net and the unilateral restructuring of Senate rules to eliminate the filibuster for judicial appointments, congressional Democrats united in opposition, moving closer to the position advocated for some time by an animated rank and file.

Strategically, it makes little sense for Democrats operating in such an environment to seek compromise and accommodation, just as it makes little sense for Democrats to continue to engage in an incremental strategy of trying to cobble together just enough votes to squeak by on Election Day. Historically, there is little reason to believe that Democrats today would be successful in their attempt to piece together 270 electoral votes or a lasting legislative majority of one or two seats. There have been six distinct political eras since Thomas Jefferson introduced political parties to national politics, and in each one the dominant party has virtually shut out its opposition. We now appear to be on the verge of the seventh, and if this is the case, then as in the past the pendulum will soon swing decisively in one direction.

Between 1800 and 1824, you had to be a Jeffersonian Democrat from Virginia to hold the White House. The Democratic Party of Andrew Jackson dominated national politics from 1828 through the Civil War, during which time the opposition Whigs were able to win only two elections, each time by nominating popular generals (who then had the bad luck to die in office). Republicans dominated the White House from Lincoln through McKinley, even though a number of elections in this period were close (Democrats actually won the popular vote in four of the nine contests from 1860 through 1892, but Grover Cleveland was the only elected Democrat during this era).

When the Republican Party realigned under McKinley, it continued to win elections, generally by wide margins; once again, only one Democrat was elected over the course of nine cycles, and Woodrow Wilson owed that victory to a split in the Republican Party. Similarly, in the nine elections between FDR's first victory in 1932 and LBJ's landslide triumph in 1964, only one Republican—Dwight Eisenhower—held the White House. The period since 1968, of course, has seen Republican dominance, including two of the most lopsided elections in history and a gradual but dramatic shift in the composition of Congress. Democrats have won the popular vote in four of the last ten elections, but claimed victory in only three, inaugurating only two presidents. It's no wonder that we look back on the eras of Jefferson, Jackson, Lincoln, and Franklin Roosevelt. These presidents ushered in partisan epochs in which their opponents were regularly vanquished.

Under the political circumstances of the post-LBJ era, it makes sense that Democrats would think it wise to cobble together enough constituent groups to cherry-pick electoral votes. It is also understandable that the method would fail. In a long arc stretching from Humphrey to

McGovern to Mondale to Dukakis to Kerry, America rejected a string of northern liberals despite the Democrats' best efforts to find the right combination of supporters at a time when liberalism itself was on the defensive. This is what minority parties do, and the results are predictable, which is why the current period holds so much promise as the terms of political discourse begin to shift.

So, it is an open question whether Bush's departure from conservative orthodoxy represents the beginning of a new era of big-government/big-business conservatism or the last stages of Republican dominance. In either case, it presents progressives with an opportunity, because the terms of political engagement are changing, while, as Jim Wallis says, the false ideological choices of the Right and Left that have defined politics for so long "have run their course and become dysfunctional." We are in a time of transition, which can only be a good thing for a party that has been losing ground under the existing system.

MARRYING MEANING AND MESSAGE

Progressives are not without resources for the coming battle. For starters, we have something to oppose. Imagine how excruciating it would be for Democrats to have to confront Bush's efforts to dismantle the signature program of the New Deal if he were coming off a forty-nine-state electoral victory like Reagan in 1984 or if he were as popular as he was in October and November 2001. But we are a long way from watching "Mission Accomplished" media events and eating "freedom fries." Instead, it is noteworthy that on the signature issues of Social Security and the Iraq war, Bush has been unable to level with the American people about what he plans to do, because it is doubtful that Americans would embrace changing Social Security if they did not believe it was irreparably broken, just as it is hard to imagine that they would have supported the invasion without believing Saddam Hussein was connected to Osama bin Laden. It is not inconsequential to the fortunes of progressives that Bush, like Professor Harold Hill in *The Music Man*, has for both issues had to whip up a false crisis in order to sell people something with dubious benefits for them. This is, of course, a time-tested method of hucksterism and its short-term effectiveness should not be underestimated. But, in the long run, it suggests that the public appetite for Bush's vision of America is limited, and this gives progressives an important opening.

Opposing an unpopular agenda is one way an opposition party can unify and find a voice. As E. J. Dionne contests, stating what you're against can bring clarity to statements of what you are for; the question of whether Democrats stand to benefit from opposing the president rather than putting forward a positive agenda, asked widely in the wake of Bush's reelection, rings hollow in the sense that successful political parties always do both. People will not vote for you simply because you're not the other guy, but strategically standing united in opposition to salient portions of the Bush agenda is the first step to communicating to voters what progressives are for by clearly showing them what progressives are against.

It also communicates strength, one of the great missing pieces of the liberal message that David Kusnet reminds us to embrace. From the height of the Vietnam War until the fall of the Berlin Wall, then again after the World Trade Center and Pentagon attacks, liberals have been on the defensive when it comes to defense. Conservatives, as noted earlier, successfully branded liberals as weak by associating them with what many saw as the excesses of the cultural turmoil of the 1960s. Nowhere has this posed a greater conundrum than at the presidential level, where voters look to their guts and ask whether they feel they can trust a candidate with their lives. It follows for many voters that someone from a "soft" party cannot be trusted, as John Kenneth White notes. A Purple Heart recipient who couched and qualified his language couldn't get it done. Especially in a television age, nothing communicates strength like simple, consistent words and actions. It is the most effective way for Democrats to combat the charge that they are weak on security issues.

This was the initial appeal of Howard Dean's presidential campaign, the willingness to speak truth to power, even to the power brokers in one's own party. Dean may have been a flawed vessel in other ways, but his outspokenness communicated moral clarity and strength in a manner not unlike George W. Bush. The Bush campaign might have had a field day questioning Dean's suitability to be president had he been the standard-bearer in 2004, but they could not have questioned where he stood or whether he could be believed. One clear message woven throughout this volume is that progressives need to speak plainly and honestly if they intend to get voters to trust them with their lives. With the ascendancy of Howard Dean to the Democratic National Committee chairmanship and the unity among congressional Democrats against Bush's Social Security plan, they are beginning to do exactly that.

Of course, what you say matters at least as much as how you say it. Progressives have been caught up in questions of what our message should be in a manner that can make you wonder whether after so many electoral beatings we know who we are. Particularly burdensome is the debate, frequently engaged in the press and on left-of-center weblogs, about whether Democrats should "move to the left" or "return to the center." By framing the discussion in this manner, progressives create a false choice. Social justice and fiscal responsibility are not left–right values. Putting aside the healthy policy differences that will and should arise naturally in any group, progressives fundamentally know where we stand.

Getting mired in an ideological contest does the work of conservatives by dividing progressives unnaturally into two camps, neither of which can win the debate. Moving to the center to reach voters in red states amplifies the sense that progressives do not know who we are and are acting out of electoral expedience. But moving to the left reinforces the sense that progressives do not reside in the mainstream. Neither is a formula for electoral success. Fortunately, it is not necessary to have this debate. Democrats can compete in the culturally conservative South without having to be beholden to cultural conservatism. The key issue is being true to our moral center everywhere.

A more fruitful discussion focuses on how progressives can develop a simple and effective brand name that plays to values with deep roots in the twentieth-century progressive movement and in the American psyche. Republicans have been so successful at branding both themselves (low taxes, values, God, strength) and Democrats (high taxes, amoral, secular, weak) that no one asks whether George W. Bush is "too conservative" for the American public or whether he "needs to move to the center." He simply represents the brand, and people give him the benefit of the doubt. This is the case despite the fact that on issue after issue, the American public is closer to Democrats (a fact that has long frustrated Democrats who cannot understand why people will not vote their interests).

John Podesta and John Halpin offer a way to do this, couched in the history of the progressive tradition but forward-looking at a time when progressives face the challenges of globalization and international terrorism. Enlisting the progressive values of fairness, global leadership, and community, they present a policy direction designed to improve living standards and economic opportunity, confront terrorism, and bring transparency to government. They propose achieving these objectives by promoting fair and responsible healthcare policies, professional development and equitable placement of teachers, energy self-sufficiency, progressive tax reform, renewed moral authority in global leadership and an integrated global/domestic approach to homeland security, free and fair trade policies, and a host of good-government measures that would embrace Craig Holman's call for closing the loophole for Section 527 organizations. Progressives of course can and should debate policy particulars, but most will probably nod their heads in agreement with the general contours of Podesta and Halpin's ideas, which can serve as a governing blueprint when the time comes and as a way of articulating a progressive vision all the time.

How that vision is articulated is a political question. Value-based solutions are prerequisite to setting the terms of political discourse, but setting the terms of political discourse requires understanding that people respond to the underlying values rather than to a laundry-list articulation of the programs and policies that progressives would enact. As George Lakoff says, most Americans want to know what you stand for and where you would lead the country rather than about your programs and plans. He suggests a simple philosophy that reflects the progressive values upon which Podesta and Halpin base their vision: a stronger America, broad prosperity, a better future, effective government, and mutual responsibility. Without principles, these are simply catch phrases, but Lakoff's philosophy is rooted in principle. As progressives embrace core beliefs and articulate a philosophy, voters will respond, as they have responded when conservatives speak of free markets, lower taxes, and smaller government.

It is also a philosophy which permits progressives to engage in and reframe the debate over cultural values that has contributed to conservative ascendancy. This point emerged time and again in this volume in different contexts. Anna Greenberg advocates reframing the cultural debate to help Democrats rebuild support among married women by speaking "in the same commonsense language moms use when they express concerns about their children" regarding drugs in school and violence in the media. John Kenneth White asserts that progressives must have a compelling values story to tell voters within the context of a traditional progressive message, and to do so we must learn to think and speak thematically rather than programmatically. Jim Wallis seeks a moral "prophetic politics"—strong on personal responsibility, opposed to corporate corruption, intolerant of the negative effects of popular culture on children, supportive of social and economic policies for the poor and working class, environmentally friendly, and multilateralist—which would link personal ethics with social justice. It would, he contends, permit progressives to articulate a vision true to our values that would resonate widely with voters who cannot place themselves easily on the existing conservative–liberal axis. And taking steps toward articulating a politics of core beliefs would redefine the way people regard those who are left of center, freeing us from the brutal stereotypes created by conservatives to undermine our ability to compete politically.

THE VIRTUE OF TECHNOLOGY—
IF WE LEARN HOW TO USE IT

As progressives move to develop a value-based brand name, technological changes are making it possible to market the brand in ways that seemed fanciful a short time ago. Weblogs, a curiosity when the 2004 presidential race began, have blended into the mainstream and are changing what it means to be a gatekeeper and journalist in a way that stands to benefit progressives. As Chris Bowers writes, blogs are virtual communities of like-minded participants that facilitate social action through discussion and debate. They operate from the bottom up, enabling anyone to initiate, investigate, or promote news stories that corporate media would normally disregard. As they grow in influence, they stretch the news agenda in ways that challenge the status quo, which is a critically important function for any group attempting to initiate widespread political change.

An argument can be made that blogs fill a need for progressives that conservatives, owing to their organization and message discipline, do not have, by providing a forum for discussion and dissemination of information while chipping away at big media influence, which has served Republicans for decades. Blogs are for progressives what talk radio is for conservatives: a medium that gives voice to the faithful. Progressives were never much good at talk radio (the recent success of Air America is a notable exception), whose big stars, like Rush Limbaugh, are able to magnify conservative anger and indignation through diatribes designed to get fists raised and heads nodding. Blogging is a more active pursuit, a chance to *make* an argument rather than just hear one.

In an age when Republicans have relied on wedge issues promulgated through television to divide the electorate, blogs bring people together, permitting far-flung, unrelated individuals with common interests to find each other. Although blogs are echo chambers for the faithful in the way that talk radio audiences are self-selecting, the Internet is a dual-influence medium in a way that radio is not, keeping an engaged group of grassroots progressives informed of a broader news agenda than what appears on the evening news, while permitting ordinary readers to shape that agenda through words and actions. Through their self-styled partisanship and self-anointed advocacy role, blogs are a high-tech throwback to the party press of the early nineteenth century. And they have moved rapidly to fill a void left by traditional journalism.

Because blogs engage people, their ability to expand and rally progressives should increase as high-speed Internet access continues to penetrate deeper into the population. Indeed, as TiVo and Internet television services blur the distinction between the two media, it is not difficult to imagine that what we recognize as television news in the years ahead will be as different from what we have today as twenty-four-hour cable news is from the days of Walter Cronkite and Chet Huntley. To the extent that this transpires, weblogs stand to increase in influence at the expense of talking-head journalism.

This would be welcome news for progressives, save for those who make their living as talking heads. Conservatives long ago figured out how to make television politics work for them by manipulating symbols and crafting talking points to set the terms of political debate. The advent of friendly outlets like Fox News powerfully enhances their ability to define the agenda. There is a reason why a majority of Americans went to the polls in 2004 holding the belief that Saddam Hussein was involved in the September 11 terror attacks, and it wasn't simply because they were not paying attention. To the contrary, they *were* paying attention. The more the Internet challenges the present shape of television news, the less television's echo chamber will have a stranglehold on the political agenda.

Having television at the center of politics has dovetailed nicely with a Republican political strategy that for the past three decades has relied in part on depressing Democratic turnout. Television is a passive, cynicism-inducing medium. It is difficult to challenge television's messages, and over time it is difficult to find the will to try. Because television naturally accentuates the part of politics that is spectacle, it treats citizens as an audience for a show rather than as participants in a process. This is particularly the case among less-well-educated individuals without the tools to yell back at the screen, voters on whom the Democratic Party has always depended. Although the ascendancy of television is not directly responsible for the decrease in turnout witnessed between 1960 and 2000, it is not surprising that the two events are correlated.

The Internet is different. It is a mobilizing medium, where heat and passion call people to action. In this regard, it has the potential to provide people with a way to reconnect with the political process in a manner that largely disappeared during the television age. Early evidence of this effect may be found in the 2004 campaign, but as Zephyr Teachout argues, the full potential of the Internet to mobilize voters remains untapped. Although the extent of that potential is open to speculation, progressives should not underestimate the importance of the Internet as a mobilization and fundraising device, or its ability to rewrite the rules of campaigning through operations that empower ordinary individuals to initiate political action.

The immediate advantages of Internet fund raising are clear, in that the Internet made the Democratic Party competitive with a well-developed, well-organized Republican fundraising apparatus. The long-term advantages of funding candidates with multiple small contributions are even more intriguing. Arguably, just as television turned politics into a show, the reliance of the parties on big contributions (largely to pay for television commercials) has served to distance regular people from the

political system. The well-documented perception that both parties respond to special-interest concerns over the interests of ordinary individuals speaks to this phenomenon.

Candidates who are funded with a mixture of large and small donations have the chance to rekindle the connection between candidate and
voter, which is vital to the health of a representative democracy and consistent with the call for campaign finance reform that Craig Holman
contends is a key component of a progressive agenda. In the short run,
this may challenge traditional ways of doing business, with the potential
to unleash a struggle between an energized grassroots contingent and
established party organizations not unlike the ongoing online battle of
words between some impassioned grassroots bloggers and the Democratic Leadership Council, where the former group sees the latter as
working toward self-preservation while blocking party reform. A similar
dynamic is evident in the Democratic Party's consultant culture of which
Amy Sullivan writes, which potentially could be challenged by fresh
blood emerging from successful campaigns spurred by grassroots support.

OUR OWN HOUSE

In order to become a vehicle for successful progressive politics, the
Democratic Party first must sort out this difficult struggle between in-
grained and emerging interests. It is a hard, painful, and necessary step,
and one that must be faced by any entrenched organization confronting
the energy and efforts of those no longer accepting of its failures. Despite all the talk of how Democrats should deal with Republicans, this
internal step may well be the most important. It is already under way;
the outcome will be a prime indicator of whether the party is prepared
to take advantage of the opportunities presented to it by Republicans.

There are many long-term benefits to displacing deep-rooted party
interests that fail to serve progressive political or policy interests. Down
the line, as progressive candidates are elected to office, grassroots connections should give progressive legislators political freedom to consider
implementing those progressive policies that in the present system
would be successfully opposed by large commercial interests. As a mat-

ter of politics and governance, the more progressives are able to harvest grassroots support, the more we will be able to shape a new political era in our own image.

A CONVERGENCE OF FORCES

Of course, the extent to which this will happen is open to speculation, but the prospects are noteworthy. Several forces are converging to create an opportunity for fashioning a progressive era:

- The end of a long period of conservative orthodoxy
- A vigorous discussion among progressives over message and voice and increased sensitivity to the language of discourse
- A renewed willingness among progressives to stand up for principle
- A political climate that should support a message of a tough internationalism in the wake of the unpopularity of the Iraq war, middle-class economic relief in the wake of rising gasoline prices and stagnant wages, fairness and responsibility in the wake of corporate greed, and political reform in the wake of congressional corruption
- The emergence of weblogs to challenge, ever so slightly, the dominance of television politics
- The dawn of a generation of socially progressive, politically engaged young voters
- Grassroots energy expressed through Internet fundraising and organizational tools

These factors reinforce each other and offer a blueprint for how progressive politics can emerge from its decades-long hiatus. And while they offer no guarantees of success, the convergence of organizational, electoral, and message opportunities bodes well for the future, if progressives approach them skillfully.

A radical band of conservatives presently hold power, but they can only continue to do so if progressives let them. When we succumb to fruitless debates about where to position ourselves on the ideological spectrum, we let them hold power. When we refuse to frame the language of political discourse on our terms, we let them hold power. When we ignore our institutional weaknesses or fail to engage the full potential of Internet, we let them hold power. When we are afraid to stand up and say who we are and what we believe, we let them hold power.

We are at a juncture in history when voters could be open to a progressive message that is thoughtfully developed and carefully delivered. It will take a lot of work to make that happen, but the blueprint for how to accomplish it is clear.

TAKING ACTION:
TALK BACK AND FIGHT BACK!

For those interested in helping bring about change, talking and taking part in new progressive media can be a prerequisite to action. Supporting emerging progressive media is without question one of the most important actions progressives can take to help build a new majority, and many emerging forms of progressive media openly encourage lively discussion, strategizing, and debate. This is particularly true on a number of rapidly growing blogs using community-based software that allows readers to talk to each other, create diaries, and reward particularly good ideas with greater exposure. These blogs also tend to be welcoming of political newcomers and of people less familiar with blogging and the Internet. To find a blog in your area, go to www.blogpac.org. Click on your home state on their interactive map.

One leading progressive blog is Chris Bowers's blog, MyDD. In addition to political and election analysis, MyDD, which stands for My Direct Democracy, features an expansive activism section. This includes a Democracy Directory, which allows people to find progressive organizations in their area, sorted by issue (labor, environment, civil rights, etc.) and group type (faith-based, neighborhood-based, age-based, etc.). Every day, MyDD features the best and most pressing action alerts submitted by its readers and highlights ongoing campaigns such as the drive to save Social Security and to create more accountability in Iraq. Beginning January 26, 2006, MyDD holds biweekly discussions on books such as this one that prescribe future plans of action to build a new progressive majority. Discussions start at 9 P.M. on the second and fourth Thursday of every month.

In addition, the Center for American Progress and its sister organization the American Progress Action Fund provide a wealth of analysis, opinion, direct action items, and progressive policy proposals on everything from achieving universal health care and restructuring secondary education to stopping genocide in Sudan and creating a more integrated national security strategy. All of the policy suggestions outlined in chapter 6 of this book are described in full detail in the Progressive Priorities section of the Center's website (www.americanprogress.org) and more direct advocacy campaigns can be found on the Action Fund's site (www.americanprogressaction.org).

The Center also provides ongoing rapid response and communications tools for progressives through its signature daily news analysis, *The Progress Report*; its Daily Talking Points e-mail; and the Center's blog, ThinkProgress.org. These products are designed to provide activists and laypersons alike with the facts, language, policy ideas, and strategies for battling the Right and advancing a more progressive America. All of the Center's products are expressly designed for public input on how best to advance a progressive agenda.

For progressive students looking for better coordination and robust intellectual debate and direct action, the Center has created a new student-based network called Campus Progress (www.campusprogress .org). Campus Progress aims to identify, train, and support progressive students and student networks across America. This past summer, Campus Progress launched the first ever National Student Conference, bringing together six hundred of the nation's leading progressive students to discuss issues; learn policy, advocacy, and media skills; and hear from a wide range of speakers, including former president Bill Clinton.

You can visit Moving Ideas (www.movingideas.org), a project of *American Prospect* magazine, to see a full list of progressive institutions and organizations focused on policy development and activism. Also, please join up with other multi-issue progressive organizations focused on policy, message, and action, including MoveOn (www.moveon.org);

Democracy for America (www.democracyforamerica.com); Campaign for America's Future (www.ourfuture.org); and People for the American Way (www.pfaw.org).

Action Plan:

Talk Back!
MyDD (www.mydd.com)

Learn More!
Center for American Progress (www.americanprogress.org)
ThinkProgress (www.thinkprogress.org)

Network with Progressive Students!
Campus Progress (www.campusprogress.org)

Find Progressive Organizations!
Moving Ideas (www.movingideas.org)

Fight Back!
American Progress Action Fund (www.americanprogressaction.org)
MoveOn (www.moveon.org)
Democracy for America (www.democracyforamerica.com)
Campaign for America's Future (www.ourfuture.org)
People for the American Way (www.pfaw.org)

INDEX

Page numbers in italics refer to figures or tables.

Perry, Bob, 114
Perry, Cindy, 48
Peter Principle, 147
Philippines, 66
Philly for Dean, 160
policy: definition of, 75;
  progressivism and, 124–25;
  religion and, 67–69, 180
political participation. *See* collective
  action
political reform, 93–98; conservative
  policies and, 94–96; progressive
  agenda for, 96–98
populism: and 1988 election, 130–31;
  using power of, 136–38
poverty, 67–68
prescription drugs, 31
Pressler, Larry, 144
programs, government, 57–58, 121,
  135
Progress for America, 115
Progressive Policy Institute, 5
progressivism: accomplishments of,
  78–79; blogs and, 170–72, 187–88;
  and campaign reform, 115–17;
  challenges for, 79–80; diversity of
  approaches in, 75–76; divisive
  issues within, 121; goals for new,
  80–98; history of, 77–79; Internet
  sites for, 193–95; issues central to,
  65; policy directions for, 124–25;
  principles of, 123–24; religious
  groups and, 70–72; ten-word
  philosophy of, 126–27; themes
  central to, 76; values of, 77–78,
  122–23, 127. *See also* Democratic
  Party
The Progress Report, 194
prophetic politics, 61, 64–65
Pryor, Mark, 142

Rassman, Jim, 53
Reagan, Ronald, 12; gender gap and,
  26; strategy of, 4, 147; and values,
  45–46, 129
realignment, 8, 16
Reed, Bruce, 96
Reich, Robert, 137
Reid, Harry, 144, 149
religion: moderate and progressive
  voices, 70–72; and new political
  option, 64, 66–73; policy making
  and, 67–69, 180; public role for,
  66–67, 72; public speaking
  references to, 139–40; values and,
  57, 63, 67–73
religious Right, 66, 70–72
Republican Party: consultants for,
  148; current situation of, 179; 527
  political organizations, 102,
  112–13; radical strategy of,
  179–81; and television, 188–89;
  2004 election dominated by, 7–8;
  and values, 45–46, 52, 53, 55
Republicans for Clean Air, 107
rights and protections, progressivism
  on, 125
Robbins, Tim, 58
Romero, Oscar, 66
Roosevelt, Franklin D., 57, 140, 182
Roosevelt, Theodore, 78
Rosenberg, Simon, 3, 147
Rove, Karl, 1, 5, 148
rural voters, 6

Salazar, Ken, 142
Sanders, Alex, 142
Scheiber, Noam, 142
Schiavo, Terri, 179
Schoen, Doug, 49
Schrader, Ginny, 167

ABOUT THE CONTRIBUTORS

Alan I. Abramowitz is the Alben W. Barkley Professor of Political Science at Emory University in Atlanta, Georgia. He received his B.A. from the University of Rochester in 1969 and his Ph.D. from Stanford University in 1976. Dr. Abramowitz has authored or coauthored four books, dozens of contributions to edited volumes, and more than forty articles in political science journals dealing with political parties, elections, and voting behavior in the United States. His most recent book, *Voice of the People: Elections and Voting Behavior in the United States*, was published in 2004.

Chris Bowers is the lead blogger for My Direct Democracy, www.MyDD.com. He has a B.A. in English from Ursinus College and an M.A. in English from Temple University, where he taught for five years and where he has completed his coursework for a Ph.D. He is on the executive committee of BlogPac.org, is a fellow at the Commonweal Institute, and has worked as a political consultant and a union organizer for the American Federation of Teachers.

E. J. Dionne writes a syndicated column for the *Washington Post* and is a best-selling author and editor of seven books on politics and public policy. A frequent television and radio political commentator, he is a senior fellow at the Brookings Institution and professor of governme at Georgetown University. He founded and cochairs the Pew Forum oɪ Religion and Public Life and is a former national political reporter for the *New York Times*.

Anna Greenberg is vice president of Greenberg Quinlan Rosner Research, a Democratic polling firm, and an adjunct professor at American University. She is a former assistant professor of public policy at Harvard University's John F. Kennedy School of Government and received her Ph.D. from the University of Chicago.

John Halpin is a senior advisor at the Center for American Progress in Washington, D.C., where he develops strategies to help build a progressive intellectual and media infrastructure. Previously, he served as a senior associate at Greenberg Quinlan Rosner Research, where he provided strategic guidance to issue organizations and national and international political campaigns, including the 2000 Gore-Lieberman campaign.

Craig Holman is currently a legislative representative for Public Citizen, where he serves as the organization's Capitol Hill lobbyist on campaign finance and governmental ethics. Previously, Holman was a senior policy analyst at the Brennan Center for Justice, New York University School of Law. He has a Ph.D. in political science from the University of Southern California.

Matthew R. Kerbel is professor of political science at Villanova University and author of five books on politics, the mass media, and the presidency, including *If It Bleeds, It Leads: An Anatomy of Television News* and the textbook *American Government: Your Voice, Your Future*. He worked as a radio and television news writer for outlets that included the Public Broadcasting Service in New York City. He received his Ph.D. from the University of Michigan.

David Kusnet served as chief speechwriter for former president Bill Clinton in the 1992 campaign and during the first two years of the Clinton administration and was a speechwriter in the presidential campaigns of Michael Dukakis and Walter Mondale. He is the author of *Speaking*

erican: How the Democrats Can Win in the Nineties and is a visiting
llow at the Economic Policy Institute in Washington, D.C.

George Lakoff, one of the world's best known linguists, is the Richard
and Rhoda Goldman Professor of Cognitive Science and Linguistics at
the University of California, Berkeley, and is a founding senior fellow of
the Rockridge Institute in Berkeley, California. He is the author of the
influential books *Don't Think of an Elephant: Know Your Values and
Frame the Debate—The Essential Guide for Progressives* and *Moral Politics: How Liberals and Conservatives Think*, as well as five other books
and numerous articles in major scholarly journals and edited volumes.

John Podesta is president and CEO of the Center for American
Progress, a nonpartisan research and educational institute committed to
developing a long-term progressive vision for America. He served as
chief of staff to President Clinton from 1998 to 2001 and as counselor to
Senate Democratic Leader Tom Daschle in 1995–1996. He is a graduate of the Georgetown University Law Center, where he is currently a
visiting professor of law.

Amy Sullivan is an editor of the *Washington Monthly*. She has written
for the *Boston Globe*, the *Los Angeles Times*, the *New Republic*, *Salon*,
and the *Washington Post*. Previously, Sullivan served as a legislative assistant to Senator Tom Daschle and as editorial director of the Pew Forum on Religion and Public Life. She holds degrees from the University
of Michigan and Harvard Divinity School.

Zephyr Teachout was director of Internet organizing for Howard
Dean's presidential campaign, where she managed the development and
deployment of tools for online political engagement. She was the founding executive director of the Fair Trial Initiative and Baobabs College
Labs, two successful nonprofits, and is currently a fellow at Harvard
University's Berkman Center for Internet and Society. She graduated
summa cum laude from Duke Law School and holds a master's degree
in political science from Duke University.

Jim Wallis, speaker, author, activist, and international commentator
on ethics and public life, is founder of Sojourners, a Christian ministry

dedicated to integrating spiritual renewal and social justice by offerii vision for faith in public life. He is editor-in-chief of *Sojourners* ma zine and was instrumental in forming Call to Renewal, a national fed ation of churches and faith-based organizations from across the theological and political spectrum working to overcome poverty. His most recent book is *God's Politics: Why the Right Gets It Wrong and the Left Doesn't Get It.*

John Kenneth White is professor of politics at the Catholic University of America in Washington, D.C. He is the author of several books, including *The Fractured Electorate: Political Parties and Social Change in Southern New England* (1983); *The New Politics of Old Values* (1988); *Still Seeing Red: How the Cold War Shapes the New American Politics* (1997); and *The Values Divide: American Politics and Culture in Transition* (2003).